P9-COP-072

WITHDRAWN

Carol Stream Public Library
616 Hiawatha Drive
Carol Stream, Illinois 60188

Praise for GirlWise

"If someone had given me this book when I was a girl, my teen years would have been decidedly less rocky!"

—Meg Cabot, bestselling author of THE PRINCESS DIARIES *series*

"This is the ultimate how-to-do-everything-right book I wish I had had growing up. From conquering math to squashing rumors, Julia courageously and gracefully leads us through that tough terrain that is teen-hood! You'll walk away with practical knowledge that will leave you more confident, ready to take on the world!"

—Isabel González, editor, "Trendspotting"
and senior associate editor, Teen People

"*GirlWise* has a closet full of good advice. Whether it's knowing how to recover from a dining disaster, becoming a true friend, managing a personal budget, or running for office, Julia DeVillers puts girls in the driver's seat. With this book by their side, girls will take giant steps toward being confident, competent and in control."

—Meg Milne Moulton & Whitney Ransome,
executive directors, National Coalition of Girls' Schools,
Concord, Massachusetts, www.ncgs.org

"*GirlWise* is more than a book—it's a tool every girl can use everyday to help her meet life's challenges, both big and small. I'll definitely be giving a copy to my 14-year-old daughter."

—Harriet Mosatche, director of Program Development,
Girl Scouts of the U.S.A., and author of
Girls: What's So Bad About Being Good? *and*
Getting to Know the Real You: 50 Fun Quizzes Just for Girls

"*GirlWise* is a triumph! This is the must-have power book for the 21st century girl."

—Emilie Davidson Hoyt, founder & president, Lather

"Filled with wise words from a slew of inspiring, wise women and girls—nothing will make you feel as confident, capable, cool, and in control as *GirlWise*!"

—Hillary Carlip, author of Girl Power: Young Women Speak Out

Contributors to Girl Wise Include

Hillary Carlip, *Girl Power* ✦ Atoosa Rubenstein, editor-in-chief of
CosmoGIRL! ✿ Nancy Gruver, publisher of *New Moon* ✦
Laura McEwen, publisher of *YM* ◉ Marci Shimoff, *Chicken Soup
for the Woman's Soul* ◉ Meg Cabot, *The Princess Diaries* ✕ Bran-
don Holley, editor-in-chief of *ELLEgirl* ✦ Isabel González, *Teen
People* ✦ Leah Feldon, *Does This Make Me Look Fat?* ✿
Carolyn Mackler, *Love and Other Four-Letter Words* ✦ Barbara
Stanny, *Prince Charming Isn't Coming* ◎ Congresswoman Deborah
Pryce ◉ Kelly Tanabe, *Get Into Any College: Secrets of Harvard Stu-
dents* ✕ Jayne Pearl, *Kids and Money* ✦ Jill Bauer, QVC host ✦
Aliza Sherman, *Cybergrrl!* ✿ Elaine St. James, *Simplify Your Life*
✦ Donna Lopiano, executive director, Women's Sports Foundation

GirlWise

How to Be Confident, Capable, Cool, and in Control

Julia DeVillers

PRIMA PUBLISHING

Carol Stream Public Library
Carol Stream, Illinois 60188

Copyright © 2002 by Julia DeVillers

All rights reserved. No part of this book may be reproduced or transmitted in any form or by any means, electronic or mechanical, including photocopying, recording, or by any information storage or retrieval system, without written permission from Random House, Inc., except for the inclusion of brief quotations in a review.

Published by Prima Publishing, Roseville, California. Member of the Crown Publishing Group, a division of Random House, Inc., New York.

PRIMA PUBLISHING and colophon are trademarks of Random House, Inc., registered with the United States Patent and Trademark Office.

Interior design by Melanie Haage.

Library of Congress Cataloging-in-Publication Data
DeVillers, Julia.
    GirlWise : how to be confident, capable, cool, and in control / Julia DeVillers.-1st ed.
        p.   cm.
    Includes index.
    Summary: A compilation of advice from the experts on topics ranging from how to host a party or wear makeup that flatters to how to change a diaper or unclog the toilet.
    Contents: Be confident – Be cool and comfortable – Be capable – Be in control – Be creative – Be caring – Be conscious.
    ISBN 0-7615-6363-6
    1. Teenage girls-Life skills guides. [1. Life skills.]. I. Title: GirlWise.. II. Title.
HQ798 .D398   2003
646.7'008352–dc21   2002070523

03 04 05 06 HH 10 9 8 7 6 5 4 3
Printed in the United States of America

First Edition

Visit us online at www.primapublishing.com

Y
646.70083
DEV

9/03

To Quinn Rachel DeVillers,
with love

Contents

Chapter 3: Be Capable

Chapter 4: Be in Control

Chapter 5: Be Creative

Chapter 6: Be Caring

Chapter 7: Be Conscious

Acknowledgments

Of course, *GirlWise* could not have been written without the generosity and incredible wisdom of the contributors. Take a few minutes and read the contributor section at the end of the book for some inside scoop on these *awesome* role models. If there's someone who really inspired you, e-mail that person or e-mail me and let us know!

Speaking of role models, a driving force behind this book is Denise Sternad, my editor. She's enthusiastic, she's smart, she's doing a *ton* for girls everywhere—and she's totally GirlWise. And thanks to the Prima and Random House team: Alice Feinstein, Libby Larson, Melanie Haage, Kristin Curtis, Jennifer Dougherty Hart, Andrea Rosen, and Andrew Stanley.

And thanks, thanks, thanks to:

The teen girls who contributed their ideas and wisdom to these pages, especially Jenny Kupper, Harmony, Joy, Megan, Lindsey, Cecily, and the Jessicas.

Susan Cohen, my fabulous agent at Writer's House. And Rebecca Sherman, her brilliant assistant.

Johannah Haney, my author's assistant. She has an incredible work ethic and a talent for doing just about anything you need her to do. Don't underestimate her role in this book.

Quinn and Jack, my amazing kids, who kept me company in my home office while I wrote this book. Jennifer Rozines Roy, my twin sister. Tons of reasons why I could thank her, but the most important is she just made me an aunt! I'm a godmother! There's Amy Rozines, my younger sister who is on her honeymoon as I write this. And my mom: Robin Rozines, always the first person to read my manuscripts.

And the DeVillers: Rene, Carol, Dawn, and Molly.

Additional thanks to: Rachael Bender, Nancy Butcher, Mary Randolph Carter Berg, Lourdes Dumke, Katie Hamilton,

Jeniffer Hankinson, Sandra Kinsler, Judge Cynthia Lazarus, Rosalie Maggio, Jorj Morgan, Jennifer Musselman, Cynthia Nellis, Monica Otero, Angela Paul, Leah Purcell, Vicki Salemi, Julie Smith, Jodi Smith, Kristy Souply, Darlene Trew Crist, Adam Roy, Kate White, Greg Roy, Jacki Watson, Roy Carlisle, Carol Burke, Geraldine Laybourne, Rachel Simmons, India.Arie, Shadow, Dr. Sylvia Rimm, and Gail Hogan.

And . . . David DeVillers, my husband. He's the BEST!

Of course I couldn't include every single topic I wanted to in this book, or it would be way too huge. If you've got a topic you want to see in a future *GirlWise* or on the Web site, e-mail me at Julia@girlwise.com or check out the Web site at www.girlwise.com.

Introducing . . . GirlWise

You walk into a crowded party. You look around. Oooookay. Where are your friends who are supposed to be here? And are NOT. Where is everyone you know?!?

What do you do?!?

You're in school giving a book report in front of the class. Suddenly everyone starts cracking up. What? What is it? You look down. One of the buttons on your shirt popped off. You are standing in front of your whole class with your bra peeking out!!

What do you do?!?

Homework, sports, social life—help!!! You've got way too much to do.

You're totally overbooked, overwhelmed, and stressed out! What do you do?!?

You feel fat.

You need a job.

You want to make a difference in the world.

You hate your clothes.

Party time! Your turn to host . . .

You're staring at your college applications, wondering if any place will accept you.

You're broke. As usual.

Life sucks. You want to be happier.

The toilet just overflowed!

You can barely carry your backpack. You wish you were stronger.

You're hanging out with celebrities and don't know what to say.

You're bored. Out of your mind.

You're at the lunch table and you've got a big hunk of salad stuck in your teeth.

What do you do when these things happen?!?

There's *so* much it would be *so* great to know. You sure don't learn it in school! You can learn some of this stuff in magazines, on the Internet, in books—but that takes some searching. And there really isn't one place, like one-stop shopping, for this kind of info. . . .

Until now! Ta-da! *GirlWise* is like the megastore of stuff you want to, you need to, you MUST know.

There are a MILLION different ways to use this book. You can read it cover to cover; you can flip to topics when you need 'em; and, of course, there are parts you'll flip to first, and parts you might skip. If you love makeup, you'll probably hit that section first. If you love sports, that's where you might think of jumping in. But I encourage you to spread your wings and take a look at things you didn't think you would like. For example, I'm not an outdoors person, but was interested when I got to interview the wilderness survival expert for this book. I never quite "got" the whole poetry thing, until I interviewed a poet for this book. Even the part on fixing the toilet—who really wants to read that, right? Well, just start to read that section . . . and I bet you will keep on reading.

I didn't know a lot of this stuff myself so I turned to the experts. More than 100 people share their wisdom in this book.

So lucky you, you're getting the inside deal on all this stuff NOW and get to know it FOREVER. Read this book, and you'll be more GirlWise.

When you're GirlWise, you are the Ultimate Teen Girl—confident, capable, comfortable, cool, crazy, and taking control of your life. No more helpless females here!

Chapter 1

Be Confident

✧ Be the Real You ✧

Girl Power! Okay, you hear that *everywhere!* But did you know that not so long ago the term didn't even exist?

Then Hillary Carlip came along with her book, *Girl Power: Young Women Speak Out.* It was one of the very first books that gave teen girls a forum to speak out. Oprah even did a whole show about it. Hillary's done other cool things, like creating VOXXY, a Web site for girls, with Jennifer Aniston, and co-authoring another book about zines with Francesca Lia Block. When Hillary was 14, she was a performer, doing things like juggling and eating fire. When she was in her teens, she started her own record label, releasing songs she wrote and performed with her all-girl band, Angel and the Reruns. She even had an international cult hit.

So you can tell Hillary Carlip is 100 percent real. When she tells you these Seven Ways to Be the Real You, listen up. She knows what she is talking about!

1. Know that you matter.

2. If you don't believe #1, then "fake it 'til you make it." Keep telling yourself, "I matter," "I'm cool," and "I'm the best" until you feel it. If *you* have total confidence in yourself, others will have it in you as well.

3. Make a list of all your kick-ass qualities—what's unique about you. *There is only one you* and that rocks! Get how *awesome* you are.

4. Then make a list of all the things you judge about yourself. You know, the negative things *you* think others think and say about you.

   Once you do that, then see how you can make those qualities cool things instead—*just cuz you say so!* For instance, wear a T-shirt that says, "I'm Fat, So What? Deal with It." Make stickers that say, "Proud to Be a Dork." Be those things with total conviction. If you make them cool qualities, *they will be!*

5. Find ways to express yourself—to show that what you have to say is important. Go online and post on message boards, start a

zine, write in a journal, do a scrapbook. Be personal; be real. Know you are helping and inspiring someone who reads what you write and realizes they are not alone.

6. Write yourself the perfect love letter—the one you'd kill to receive from someone else—going on and on about how AMAZING you are. Then mail it to yourself. When you're feeling down, unconfident, or just plain crappy, take it out and read it.

7. Make one more list. Answer the following questions (and others): If there were no judgment from anyone else, no one to laugh at you, tease you, or make fun of you . . .

What would you be?

What would you do?

How would you dress?

(etc.)

Then bit by bit, start moving toward the real you. You *can* do it!!

❧ Be Your Own Best Friend ❧

BFF. When you read that, Best Friend Forever, who are you thinking of?

Well, wait just one second. Atoosa wants you to think of *yourself.*

Presenting: Atoosa Rubenstein, editor-in-chief of *CosmoGIRL!* In her own words:

> It's funny. Sometimes we girls find ourselves thinking things like: How can I be a better friend? A better girlfriend? A better daughter? How can I make people love me? Accept me? As an editor of a teen magazine, these are the questions my readers ask me every day. But it all comes down to one thing: For all those *other* relationships to fall into place, one particular relationship has to be super-tight: your relationship with yourself.
>
> If it sort of sounds like blah-blah, believe me, I understand. But it's for real.

The better you treat yourself, the better everyone will treat you. Know that every single person you meet looks to you to set the boundary as to how they're going to treat you. If you find that you're always being dogged by guys, you need to look at yourself and how much you're expecting from these guys. Chances are you expect very little.

How good your relationship with yourself is directly affects the value you place on yourself, and that's what every single person you meet will go by. Treat yourself like the most precious possession in your life, and you'll find that others will treat you the same. How genius—*you* set the rules! Yes, that's how it's been all along. You just hadn't been setting rules and instead were letting others set them for you.

When you pass by a mirror, listen for your inner voice. Mine always says something like, "Hey, gorgeous!" How about yours? If it says something positive, something loving, then you *are* being a good friend to yourself. If it says something mean or degrading like, "Ugh, what a big butt!" or "My hair is frizzy again!" that's okay, too. It's just that we've got work to do together. Don't beat yourself up about beating yourself up. The glass is half full, CosmoGIRL! The glass is half full. Just know that you've got a goal and need to map out a way to get there. And remember, my friend, that your game plan is not about getting liposuction or extensions so you look like a shampoo ad (hello? retouching!?). The goal is to train yourself to see your own tush as luscious and curvy and your own hair as exotic and wild. Come on—can you even *think* of a more special and delicious person than you? No way!

Another quick test: Since we're all friends here, we can admit that we've all been in a situation where we've liked a guy and, well, let's just say it was unrequited. Ask yourself, why didn't that guy like me? If your answer is anything other than "Because that guy clearly had no *taste*," then we need to talk. Okay, so maybe I'm exaggerating a *little*, but you know what I mean.

Think about it. If some guy didn't like your very best friend back, what would you tell her? That maybe it was because her skin is too broken out? No way, because you know what a jewel she is, and anyone who doesn't see that as well just doesn't deserve to know her. And who really *is* your very own best friend? You, of course! So there! Believe it, girl, because you are *that* special. It's true. There's *no one* more special than you. Always remember that.

I know you believe me, sister. You're just wondering *how*? How can I have a love affair with myself?? Cosmo-GIRL! to the rescue!"

Date yourself. Do for yourself the nice things you'd do for a guy you really wanted to make fall in love with you. Buy yourself thoughtful gifts (like a beautiful book of poetry or an adorable pedicure set); bake yourself your favorite goodie; take yourself places you've always wanted to go. (Who cares if no one but you wants to go to the Museum of Natural History? Go solo! Can you imagine better company?)

Indulge yourself. Take at least one night every week and do something that's totally all about *you*. (I know, I know—you're busy! But if your friend or a guy asked you to hang out one night this week, you'd figure out a way, right? Do the same for your precious *self!*) Play your most favorite music (current or an old favorite), or do like me and play really relaxing New Age music and take a really sudsy, yummy bubble bath and have a spa night. Light an aromatherapy candle and do your nails, deep condition your hair, deep breathe, and just be.

> **Keep your head high and shoulders back. It will make you feel—and look—more confident.**
> —Cecily, 14, California

Compliment yourself. How much do we love it when someone tells us that our outfit looks great or that we have beautiful eyes, right? Well, why wait until someone *else* makes your day? Plant yourself love letters in your room, your locker, anywhere you can. And create a big sign to hang on your bathroom or bedroom mirror that says, "Gosh, you are BEAUTIFUL!"

Inspire yourself. I can't think of anyone who doesn't have a tough day every so often. But when you're having one of those moments, it can feel as though you're the only one in the whole world who's ever been that low. But you're not. Read empowering stories about amazing women, women of strength. And remember that each one of those amazing women, from Rosa Parks to Madonna to Sally Ride, all started in the very same place you did. Remind yourself of the amazing things you can do! It's like watering the plant of your life. (It's thirsty!)

❀ Make Your Voice Heard ❀

Someone is ragging on you and you want her to cut it out—NOW!

There's a cause that you feel totally passionate about, and you want to stand up for it.

You've got an idea for a new way of doing something.

That's right—you've got something to say! So what's holding you back from speaking out?

Nancy Gruver, founder and publisher of *New Moon* magazine, which publishes what girls have to say, says this:

One of the common fears girls have is using their voices. There's the fear of being embarrassed. There's the worry that people will disagree with you. That they'll dismiss what you're saying as not important. That they'll laugh at you. And you know what? Those things *will* happen sometimes. But it doesn't mean you should stop speaking. It also doesn't mean the views of those people are right!

If you've got something to say, don't hold it in. Speak out. Make your voice heard. Things never change if we all stay quiet. Girls and women make up more than 50 percent of this world. We have a real responsibility to share our feelings and our reality. And girls have a lot of good ideas and important things to say—if only they would say them. If thoughts stay only in our heads, we can't make the world better. The world is missing out on our creativity, our good ideas, our energy.

It's an incredible gift that girls bring to the world when they are willing to speak out. And when you speak out, you feel stronger. You know what? You actually are stronger.

Nancy also has some ways you can feel more confident about making your voice heard.

Write down what you think you want to say. Put your words on paper before you have to speak them. Nothing long (it's not a school paper!), but just your thoughts on the page. Read over what you have written. Ask yourself if it explains what you want it to explain. Think about what's most important for you to express and then write from the heart.

Ask someone to read what you've written. Choose someone whose opinion you trust, such as a teacher, a caring friend, or a parent. Ask for that person's thoughts. Sharing what you write helps you get really clear on what you want to say. It can prepare you to hear what other people's reactions might be. And then you can make any changes you want.

Determine who you want to hear it. Who will your audience be? Is it something you want to say to your teacher? To someone who is bothering you? To your classmates? To your community in a letter to the editor of your local paper?

What do you want to have happen? What result do you want after you speak out? The results can range from very personal to worldwide. Do you want someone to stop doing something to you? Do you want it published on a Web site? Do you want other people to change their opinions?

Figure out the best way to make your voice heard. Thinking about your audience and the results, what would be the best way to get your message across? Would it be to tell someone to her face? To write an article for your school newspaper? A letter? An e-mail?

◉ Love Your Looks ◉

We've all done it. Picked up a magazine, flipped through it, looked at the photos of all the models and actresses, then compared ourselves to all the thin, supposedly perfect girls . . . and felt really, truly inferior.

Laura McEwen, publisher of *YM* magazine, one of the top teen magazines in the world (who's been there herself) says this:

> I had a gorgeous mother. It was daunting. To make myself feel better, and to help sort out my identity, I used to cut out pictures in magazines of all the models I wanted to look like. Anything seemed better to me than me.
>
> Teens have an infusion of images that say you have to be so thin; they see them on TV, in magazines, on billboards, everywhere they look. Most teens have concerns about their changing appearance at some point, which is normal. Some girls snap out of it and move on. But many others get caught until it gets out of control. Their entire lives center on being thin and on dieting. I have personally known so many young women who have issues with eating—neighbors, relatives, friends in various stages of recovery from eating disorders. And they all began in their early teens.
>
> I'm proud to say that at *YM* magazine, our editorial team (led by Christina Kelly) has taken a stand. *YM* is now promoting a variety of looks—different girls, different shapes, different sizes—in the pages of our magazine. We want to send the message that all appearances are to be admired, and will no longer promote dieting to our readers. And the response has been overwhelmingly positive from teens and their mothers; women from all over the country have written to express gratitude and admiration.

Laura's goal is to send an important message: "Love yourself. Feel beautiful all the time, no matter what your shape or size or ethnicity. Love yourself because you are worthy of it." Here's how she suggests you start:

Talk to yourself in a positive way. Look in the mirror. Smile and laugh and say out loud, "I am beautiful." Feel a little stupid doing that? Do it anyway!

Disregard negative messages from your parents about your body. This is a touchy subject, but an important one. Some parents send messages to their daughters, through words and non-verbal behaviors, that they don't think their daughter's bodies are okay. Fathers in particular play an important role in a teen girl's self-esteem. If your dad makes comments or puts you down about your weight, diet, or your body, don't let it get to you. Tell your parents to worry about their own bodies, and—unless a doctor is concerned—not about yours.

Find hobbies that shift your focus. If you're bored and hanging out with nothing to do, you're more likely to have time to obsess about food and dieting. Try some activities that make you feel good about yourself. Get involved in sports and outdoor activities or volunteer and feel good about helping others.

Remember that actresses and models have insecurities, too. Given the fact that they have hairdressers, makeup artists, and lighting people making them look camera perfect, they should feel less-than-perfect, too.

So, should we all just accept what we see? Should we just think, "Oh well, there isn't much we can do about it!"? Nope. Listen to Laura:

> When someone compliments you, just smile and say, "Thank you!"
> —Ellie, 14, New York

Take a stand. Help promote the idea that size shouldn't matter. Write and e-mail magazine editors, your favorite celebrities, and modeling agencies. Ask them straight out: Why are you only showing girls who are so thin? The media and decision makers need to hear more from girls. Sure, girls won't be able to make the pursuit of unrealistic beauty go away forever; society will always have its ideals. But you do have a chance to moderate it and make it less of a big deal.

Laura tells this story: "A reporter called to ask if *YM* was worried about showing heavier models, less traditional models. Were we worried that we are glamorizing their imperfections?

"I answered: 'What imperfections?'"

◎ Deal with Embarrassment ◎

Walking into the guys' bathroom!

Toilet paper sticking to the bottom of your shoe on the dance floor!

Vomiting on your crush!

Most embarrassing moments! I love to read them in magazines. Who doesn't? They're funny and, best of all, they happened to somebody else!

Admit it, though, you've had some of your own. Take a moment to think about a time when you totally humiliated yourself. Is your face red yet?

Okay, now take a minute to think about how you handled it. Because how you react *afterward* is what's really going to make it worse for you, or make it into—yes—a *positive* experience.

Sherrie Krantz is the person behind the Web site, Vivian Lives.com. Vivian is a cartoon character whom you follow around in her glam life. And even though she's glam and hip, she also embarrasses herself a lot. And Sherrie confesses that some of those embarrassing moments Vivian faces are based on, yup, personal experience. Sherrie says:

> Vivian is very klutzy and has these humiliating moments that you read about on the site. Like she is always walking right out of her shoes and tripping and falling on her face. Or she's walking down the street, drinking her latte. And people are checking her out, looking at her and smiling, so she's thinking she must be looking really good. And then she realizes that there's a hole in her cup and all the drink is spilling down the front of her outfit. Of course, *that's* what everyone is smiling about so the joke's on her.

Here's what Sherrie says to do in a red-faced moment:

Remember that it happens to everyone. We've all been there. Embarrassing moments happen to every single person.

Laugh. You have to laugh. Come on, if this was happening to someone else, you would be cracking up, wouldn't you? So laugh at yourself.

Don't overreact to it. But don't laugh too hard, or people will think you're desperate. Don't cry, don't run away, don't scream: "I can never be seen in public again!" Then people will think your goof is worse than it is, and they'll either laugh at you when you're gone or feel sorry for you.

But don't try to act *too* cool about it. Say that you totally fall on your face and pretend you didn't do anything. Well, people will be laughing about it behind your back later. Instead, encourage them to laugh *with* you by saying something like, "Did you see me just fall on my face?!?! Can you believe I did that?!"

Get over it. Don't keep bringing it up, except maybe as a good story to tell once in a while.

Sherrie says: If you handle your embarrassment well, you come off as someone who:

has a good sense of humor,

is confident, and

doesn't take life too seriously.

Sounds good, huh?

(That list at the start of this section? Every single one of those experiences happened to me. But hey, I'm over them. Really, I am; totally. Okay, maybe not the throwing up on my crush part. I wonder if he still remembers that, wherever he is. Like he might turn on the TV and see me on Oprah talking about this book and say, "Hey! I know her! She puked on me!" I was just getting over the stomach flu, okay? I'm done. It's over. Let's move on. . . .)

> **Laugh at yourself. If you're laughing, too, then no one can laugh at you; they can only laugh with you.**
>
> —Allison, 17, Texas

✖ Improve Your Self-Esteem ✖

How's your self-esteem today?

Yeah, yeah, I know. Sounds like something you hear in school all the time during Good Character Week or whatever. Self-esteem *is* kind of a buzzword now. You might hear about it so much that you are ready to tune this out. But wait, come back for a second . . .

What does self-esteem *really* mean? Self-esteem is having confidence in and satisfaction with yourself. You're proud of yourself, you feel good about yourself, you like yourself. What's important to know is that true self-esteem comes when you are thinking and acting in ways you can be proud of, when you are comfortable with yourself from within.

Marci Shimoff is the co-author of *Chicken Soup for the Woman's Soul, Chicken Soup for the Mother's Soul 1 and 2,* and *Chicken Soup for the Single's Soul.* More than 12 million copies of her books have been sold. She also owns a company called the Esteem Group. Yup, esteem as in self-esteem. Marci admits this: "I didn't have high self-esteem growing up. But I wanted it. I started going to workshops on self-esteem. I read books on how to get it and used what worked for me."

The way to get this inner feeling of self-esteem is to focus on your whole self—your body, your mind, and your spirit. And here are nine things Marci found really work.

1. **Talk to yourself—and be nice.** Whether you have high or low self-esteem is based on your self-talk. You have 60,000 thoughts running through your head all day. And 95 percent are the same thoughts that ran through your head yesterday. And for most people, 80 percent of them are negative. You put yourself down. You think, "I'm stupid. I can't do this."

   Our words and thoughts create chemicals in our bodies. These chemicals influence your health and how you feel! Positive thoughts are real medicine.

   So the place to start is to *notice* what you say to yourself then *stop saying words that weaken you,* such as:

- can't

- have to

- should

Anytime you say those kinds of words, you weaken yourself. Here are examples of negative thoughts:

- I am stupid.

- I am fat.

- I am worthless.

"I am" is the most powerful phrase in our language. You can switch the negative words from above around and have the opposite effect:

- I *can* do it.

- I am a *good* person

Much better.

2. **Avoid toxic people.** Toxic people are those who criticize, gossip, and generally drag you down. You're influenced by what other people around you say. No matter how strong you are, their messages still get inside and affect you. Instead, spend time with people who are nurturing, nourishing, and supportive, and who encourage you to be who you really are. (Ooh, this is a good one. See the sections about Gossip and Put-Downs in chapter 6 for more!)

3. **Be active physically.** Move your body. When you feel good physically, you feel good emotionally. Exercise gives you a "high" from chemicals called endorphins. When you exercise, you start a chain reaction that causes you to feel good about yourself.

4. **Drink lots of water.** Water flushes all the toxins (the bad stuff) out of your body. When you don't drink enough water, you feel tired and sometimes depressed. Drink eight to ten glasses of water a day.

5. **Get enough sleep.** Research shows that our bodies work in what is called circadian cycles. When we sleep when nature

sleeps, our bodies respond. Every hour before midnight gives you sleep that's twice as good as the hours you sleep after midnight. So sleeping from 10 P.M. to 6 A.M. is better than midnight to 8 A.M. even though it's the same number of hours.

6. **Have a connection to a higher power.** If you were to interview people who have high self-esteem, you'd find that they tend to have a feeling of connection to something that is bigger than themselves. They might call this power God, a Source, or a universal energy. When you feel you are part of a bigger whole, when you feel connected, you have a sense of purpose in your life. Being out in nature can help you connect. Prayer also can be immensely helpful.

7. **Meditate.** I find that meditating 15 to 20 minutes a day improves self-esteem. Meditation helps you think more clearly, be more creative and energetic, and feel more peace inside. I started meditating when I was 16, and it changed my life.

8. **Give thanks.** I recommend doing a gratitude exercise. This is one of the best ways I know to build self-esteem. It gets you in the habit of looking at your life as a glass that is half full and not half empty, which helps you be optimistic. Each night think of or write down five things you are grateful for that happened that day. For example:

"I'm grateful that I had a great time with my friends today."

"I'm grateful that I felt healthy."

"I'm grateful that I watched a beautiful sunset."

"I'm grateful that I didn't have to worry about not having food to eat today."

"I'm grateful that I stood up for myself in gym today."

Do this for twenty-one days. That's the amount of time it takes to establish a new habit, so you are more likely to continue.

9. **Listen to your inner voice.** Each of us has an inner knowing in our heart, in our solar plexus, that we often ignore. When you aren't feeling good about yourself, or when you have a problem, let your inner voice speak to you.

Before you go to sleep at night, put a pad of paper and pen by your bed. Say aloud or think to yourself: "I don't know what to do about (the problem). I want to have an inner sense of what to do."

Then go to sleep. As soon as you wake up, write your thoughts down on the paper. Don't judge what you write. Don't criticize yourself for what you write. Don't let the pen stop. It's giving you a message from your inner voice. Have the courage to listen to that message. You'll discover what's best for you.

Marci recommends that you pick one of these exercises and do it for a month. Then pick another until you have tried all of them. After nine months, you will notice how good you feel about yourself. Nine months seems like a long time—well, okay, it is; but it's not so long if you think about how it will make the REST OF YOUR LIFE better!!!

❖ Look Confident ❖ (Even If You're Faking It)

You have to give an oral report in front of your class.

Your crush is heading toward you . . . here he comes . . . closer . . . closer . . .

You're heading into an interview for your first job.

You *want* to look confident. Like it's no big deal. You're in total control, very coooool.

But nope. You feel nervous. Self-conscious. Really, really dumb—like the biggest idiot in the universe.

Hey, you know what? You can fake self-confidence—and they'll never know.

Sherry Maysonave is going to tell you how to look confident even when you not feeling it. She's the president of Empowerment Enterprises and author of *Casual Power: How to Power Up Your Nonverbal Communication and Dress Down for Success.* Here's what Sherry says:

Perform a simple little magic trick in your mind. It's called the "It's Showtime—Lights, Camera, Action" magic trick. It's a popular secret with successful actors, speakers, athletes, singers, and performers of all types. Just follow these steps:

Step 1: Choose your scenario.

This magic trick begins in your mind. You pretend you are the person who would best get through the situation. Say you're nervous about your tennis tournament. Pick out your favorite tennis champ and be her. Or you're nervous about talking to the new guy in school. Pretend you're a celebrity whom everyone adores. *(I'm going to try this! I will be Gwyneth Paltrow. No, Jennifer Aniston—that's who I'll be because then, of course, I get to walk in with Brad Pitt!)*

Step into the character of your choice in your mind *first*. Stay with this for a few seconds, minutes, or long enough to let the feeling of it wash over you. Tell the self-conscious or nervous part of you goodbye, you'll see that part of you later.

Step 2: Get into the role physically.

Silently say these words to yourself and say them with enthusiasm, "(Your Name), it's SHOWTIME! Now hit it! LIGHTS! CAMERA! ACTION!!!" and instantly become the confident you. Allow your body to shift, standing tall and proud.

You can train your body to quickly respond to the "It's Showtime" command by practicing these *I-Am-Confident* looks, postures, and actions:

- Stand tall, with your shoulders back.

- Hold your head high as if it is attached to the ceiling by a string that will not let you look down or let your shoulders droop.

- Smile. If that's asking too much, then just hold your mouth slightly open in a pleasant expression. Tight lips are a dead giveaway of hidden nervousness or upset.

- Look people in the eye. Making eye contact and maintaining it projects ultimate confidence. It also conveys trustworthiness.

Find Your Power Stance

Sherry says you can tap into your own confident power, by finding your personal "Power Stance." Stand with your feet slightly apart, several inches. Try your feet in varying placements, never more than a few inches apart, until you feel a sense of strength in your lower body. That is your personal Power Stance! Memorize it. Then practice standing in that stance for 5 minutes (or longer) at a time, several times a week. Keep your feet flat on the floor. Don't lock your knees, but stand straight with your head up, looking outward. Do this by a window where you can see out or find something else to look at (other than TV). While your eyes are looking ahead at the object of your choice, focus your mind all the way down to your feet. Feel how strong you become! This inflow of strength is available to you at any time. Feeling your own power is serious business. With consistent practice, your genuine confidence will soar.

- Keep your hands away from your clothing (no fidgeting, tugging, or pulling!). Also keep your hands away from your face, your mouth (no nail biting!), and your hair. Excessive touching or twirling of the hair denotes nervousness or emotional upset.

- Stand firm. If you shift your feet around or from side to side when standing, you are saying on the nonverbal level that, inside, you do not feel confident or comfortable with yourself. How we stand affects how we feel about ourselves and how others perceive us, especially our confidence level.

- Sit tall, if you are required to sit. Confidence doesn't publicly slump or attempt to lie down in a chair. Slide your rear all the way to the back of the chair with your back flat against the chair back; this will require you to sit up straight without slumping your shoulders.

☀ Survive a Party ☀ When You Don't Know Anyone

"My cousin's having a big party," your BFF told you. "She said I could bring someone. Meet you there. I'll get there before you."

You got the parents' okay. You got the outfit, the hair, the makeup. Everything's smooth. You walk in the front door and see the party's jumpin'. You look around for your BFF . . . and look . . . and look. No sign of her. Who are these people? You don't know *anyone*. You check the address—yup, you're at the right place. Scan again. Not one single person you recognize.

Okay, do you run the other way? Hide in the bushes until BFF arrives? Keep standing there like a loser? No thanks.

Really, it's *not* true that everyone is staring at you. They're busy trying to have a good time themselves. But when you feel self-conscious, it can feel like everyone is looking at you. And who knows, some cute guy might really be looking at you. So let's pull this off.

Step 1: Make an entrance.

First, get your panic under control. Stop thinking, "I don't know anyone! I will be left standing by myself, and everyone will be staring at me wondering who the Outcast is." Think instead, "Look at all the new people I get to meet. Since they don't know me, they don't know that I am shy or not Miss Popularity at school. So I can be the Social Butterfly here."

Act. Imagine you are your absolute favorite actress. The one you just know could waltz into a party and feel at ease. Pretend you are making your way onto the red carpet at the MTV awards. Stand like she would. Hold your head up like she would.

Put a smile on your face. It will look like you are having a good time already.

Pretend you see someone you know. Look over the crowd. Make your eyes light up and smile bigger as if you are oh-so-thrilled to see these people. Start walking like the actress would, right into the party.

Walk in. Walk right to . . . (choose one of the following:)

> Don't change the way you are just to make others like you. They should like you for *you*, and that's all that matters.
>
> —Melissa, 12, Arizona

- **Option 1: the bathroom.** It gives you a place to go to calm your nerves. It gives you a place to go check your hair, your makeup, and that smile you plastered on. It also gives you a place to Go . . . (hey, being nervous can do that to a girl!).

  Don't know where the bathroom is? Not a bad thing—that gives you a reason to wander around looking like you really have somewhere to be, someone who is waiting in suspense for you to return. If you don't have any luck finding it, ask someone who looks approachable. Obviously, a female is recommended for that delicate question. (Hey, now you've talked to one person! That's a start.) Once you're in there, don't stay too long.

- **Option 2: the food and drink place.** Go get a drink (but nothing with alcohol, which can cause you to do something embarrassing). Stay in control. Grabbing a soda will give you something to do with your hands other than resort to habits such as playing with your hair, which give away the fact that you're nervous. If there's food, you probably won't want to take any yet. If you are standing there by yourself and eating, it will be obvious that you are all alone.

Sneaky Hint: Grab two drinks. Then it will look as though you are getting a drink for someone else, too. That makes it look like you know someone there and aren't all alone. Get it? Then, as you are wandering around, people will assume you are bringing a drink to someone.

Try to make conversation with somebody near you, such as the girl in line behind you, while you are getting the drink. You're not coming off as desperate, just friendly. Try to think of something to start that conversation that will help you see whether she has Rescue Me potential. For example:

"I'm dying of thirst. I went for a run before this and totally overdid it."

"I love your earrings. Where did you get those? They would look great with the T-shirt I got at the concert last week."

Hopefully, she'll pick up your cues and respond. If not, oh well. Not everyone is as socially skilled as you are. So if she just sort of says, "Yeah" and gets her drink, don't let it throw you. It's her loss.

Step 2: Walk around.

Still no sign of BFF or a familiar face? Walk around the room. Try to look like you aren't anxious, but are content to just hang out by yourself for a minute until you return to all the people who are dying to hang with you, la-la-la.

While you are walking anywhere, make eye contact with people. Say "hi" as you walk by, even if you don't know them. You'll look confident—and approachable. And when you get people to smile and say "hi" back, you will feel better.

Step 3: Find the host.

Look for the person who is throwing the party. Or ask someone where she is. Wait until she is not deep in conversation with anyone then say, "Hey, great party. I'm your cousin's friend, (your name). Have you seen your cousin?"

You can get a feel for how friendly she is from there. If she says, "Nope" and turns back to her crowd, then there you go. Don't feel stupid; she's the one who needs Hostess Lessons. Or she might start talking to you, and you can throw yourself at her mercy. Casually go, "Ack, I don't know anyone here." And she can introduce you to someone to talk to.

Step 4: Find someone else by themselves.

Best bet is to choose a girl for this one. Better to avoid talking to guys you don't know when you don't know who's who yet. Casually walk over and say hi. Don't hang on her. Say something like, "I can't find my best bud anywhere. Do you see a girl with black hair down to here . . . ?" or "Do you know what time it is? I think my friend is late." You have established you are not a geek with no friends. And if she has no one to hang out with, she can help you in your mission and give you someone to talk to. (Don't use and abuse her though. If your BFF shows up, don't blow this new girl off. Introduce her to your BFF and remember how it feels to be alone. Let her hang with you guys if she seems to want to.)

Sneaky Cell Phone Trick: Go out on the front steps or yard where you can see when your BFF arrives. Call a friend or your mom on the cell and talk to them for a while. Or even fake it and pretend you're talking on your phone. You'll look like you got torn away from having a great time at the party for an important call instead of just standing around the party feeling out of it.

(Turn it OFF, first, though! My assistant Johannah just told me that when she did this, her cell phone started ringing so everyone knew she was faking it. So turn it OFF, first!)

Step 5: Last-ditch effort.

Okay, say you are still feeling really dumb being at this party alone. You shouldn't be, you know, but you are. Got a cell phone? If you can reach her, call your BFF and find out her ETA (estimated time of arrival). No cell phone? Ask to use the host's phone. It's okay to ask to use someone's phone! Just don't hang on it too long in case they don't have call waiting.

What if your BFF is a no-show? Being GirlWise means always having a backup plan before you get to the party for situations like this. What if the party isn't your style, or gets out of hand? Make sure you know how to reach your parents for a ride home. Or call a cab. Don't stay somewhere you feel uncomfortable. Thank the host and take off. And hope for a Better Party Next Time. . . .

❀ Say Hi ❀
. . . and Have Them Say Hi Back!

You're new at school and don't know anyone.

You've got a crush on the guy who sits next to you in math . . . but you've never said one word to him.

That girl in your youth group has Friend Potential.

Great things can start with one simple word: hi.

That seems like it should be easy, right? But I know, I know, it's not. Just opening your mouth to say that one word can make you a nervous wreck, make you worry that you'll look dumb, make you afraid they are going to look at you and laugh in your face or something.

Susan Haworth produced a radio feature called PowerTalk, where she interviewed all kinds of people about what makes them feel comfortable talking to other people.

"It doesn't matter how old you are," she says. "Approaching someone you don't know can be intimidating." Here's what Susan suggests you do to increase your chances for the best response:

Approach the person when he or she is alone. Here's why this is important: First of all, if someone is standing or seated alone, that person is usually very grateful to have someone with whom to talk. And probably happy *not* to have to make the first move. Second, you never know what you may be interrupting when you approach two or more people talking; it could be a private conversation. Finally, groups do strange things to people. Sometimes people feel as though they have to react a certain way in front of others—for example, show they are cool and you're not. Get a person away from a crowd and chances are that individual will be more relaxed and receptive.

I've been told over and over again, the *absolute* best way to break the ice for social purposes is a *genuine* compliment such as:

- "I really like your sweater."

- "That's a great color on you."

- "You gave a great speech."

- "I like your haircut."

Introduce yourself. After the person says thanks (for the compliment), you can introduce yourself and maybe start up a conversation. Hard as it is to believe, almost everyone has a streak of shyness that prevents him or her from initiating a conversation with strangers. When you're the one who takes the first step, your future friend will be forever grateful *and* you'll feel more confident every time you do it. As the old saying goes: A stranger is just an unmet friend.

Your very best friendships ever can start with that one word: hi.
(Okay, trust me, I'm not Miss Susie Sunshine thinking every "hi!" results in immediate bonding. There's always a chance you could get rejected, that the response to your "hi" could be "buh-bye." Sure, that would suck. But if you think you can't hack that, go jump to page 209 and read "Deal with Rejection," and hey, you'll have all bases covered!)

❀ Recover from Dining Disasters ❀

Your crush invited you to dinner with his parents.

Your mom's boss invited your family out to a restaurant. Mom has a "Don't embarrass me" look on her face.

Prom time! All dressed up and going out to dinner before the dance.

Feeling just a little Pressure, or what? These are the times when Dining Disasters happen. Something on your plate is totally unrecognizable. You spill your drink all over the table. Eat something gross. Get something huge stuck in your teeth. You burp.

Are you totally horrified? Are you doomed to dine alone? Nyah. These things happen—to everyone. What counts is how you react to them.

Ellen Kaye is a presentation and etiquette coach. One of her specialties is teaching people how to survive meals with style. She says no matter what goofs you make along the way, it's how you handle them afterward that others will remember.

When you're GirlWise, you're the Ultimate Dining Chick: polished, classy, gracious—even when you goof. Ellen will now tell you how you can pull it off:

Disaster 1: You eat something gross.

Oh, *disgusting!* You just ate a hunk of gristle—you know, that fatty part of the meat that is about to make you gag. First of all, don't gag or announce you have something gruesome in your mouth. Try to get through this while calling as little attention to yourself as possible. It would seem logical to just spit it out into your napkin, right? Wrong.

If you spit it into your napkin, when you have to use your napkin later you might wipe that chewed-up morsel right onto your face. Now that would be less than attractive. The etiquette for dealing with gross gristle is to:

1. Lift your napkin up and cover your mouth almost to your nose.

2. Take your fork and lightly spit the chunk on to it. (What goes in with your fork, goes out with your fork.)

3. Place it on your plate in the place others will least likely see it. Try to disguise it with a piece of parsley or bread or something.

4. Ignore it.

Disaster 2: You spill your drink all over everything.

Spillage! You knocked over your glass. What do you do? Scream? Hide under the table? No!

Rule number one: Stay calm. Don't call too much attention to it. Here's your attitude: "Oh, oops, but no biggie."

Use your napkin to mop it up. Apologize once to everyone. Ask the host for more napkins and help her clean it up. She'll say, "Don't worry about it." So, stop worrying about it! Move on, and everyone else will, too.

What if your drink was bright red and spilled all over someone's clothes? Tell her that you are really sorry, you feel terrible about it, it was a clumsy accident. Offer to pay to have it dry cleaned (one or two nights of babysitting should cover the cost). If she is GirlWise, she will remember that Accidents Happen, and you'll be forgiven.

Disaster 3: You get a hunk of food stuck in your teeth.

Yum, veggie pizza. You take a bite. Then you get a giant wad of spinach stuck in your teeth. You just know it is there. And it is huge and ugly.

- Don't smile at your crush.

- Swipe your napkin over your teeth.

- If it's still stuck, don't rub your tongue around your mouth to try to get it out. It looks really bizarre. Excuse yourself to go to the bathroom to remove it.

Hint: Set up a Teeth Check! Think of a secret signal in advance with your buds. Cup both hands around your mouth as though you're scratching your nose. Grin really wide so only she can see. Have her nod "yes" for "all clear," or "no" for "quick, to the ladies room!"

DON'T	DO
Chew with your mouth open so everyone can enjoy the view.	Swallow your food before you talk.
Inhale your food. *Oink!*	Eat at about the same pace as the other people.
Put your elbows on the table. (Your mother was right.)	Put your napkin on your lap.
Play with your hair. No one wants hair falling into the food. (Ick!)	Say "excuse me" if you have to leave the table, then leave quietly.
Rock back on your chair legs. (Boom. Ouch!)	Sit up straight.
Kick the table leg. (Might be a person's leg. Another ouch!)	Keep your feet on the ground.

(I was invited to a senior prom when I was a sophomore. So I'm sitting at the pre-prom dinner table with about five other couples, feeling all cool. And suddenly I became a Double Dining Disaster. My steak had all these fatty parts, and I ate one that was like rubber. I'm chewing for about an hour, I think, and getting nowhere. I can't swallow it, and I don't know what to do with it.

At the same time, I'm trying to look like everything is fine, no prob, so I'm sawing away at my steak. It's so fatty, though, that my knife won't go through it. And it flies *off* my plate and across the table into the lap of the senior sitting opposite me. It *also* knocked over her soda glass on the way. So there she is, in her gorgeous prom dress—covered in soda and with a steak in her lap. What could I say? Nothing since I'm choking on that hunk of gristle.)

My face is bright red just *writing* that. I can't believe I shared that story.

◎ Fail ◎

That's right: Fail!

What? Being GirlWise means failing? Do I mean I am giving you permission to fail your tests at school? Am I saying you should give up?

Of course not! But I *am* saying that you need to accept that every now and then, you *will* make a mistake. You will try something, and you will fail.

Fawn Germer interviewed women for her new book, *Hard Won Wisdom.* Oscar winners, CEOs, Nobel Peace Prize winners, the president of Switzerland—she talked to them all. Fawn found out that they all talked about the importance of failing once in a while. Here's her advice:

> Every-
> body makes
> mistakes.
> —Chante, 14,
> Nevada

Be okay with failure. Failure is not a bad thing. If you aren't failing every once in a while, you aren't pushing yourself. You have to fail a little to find out your limits. And also to learn what you can do differently next time.

Say you're thinking about taking that Advanced Calc class because it sounds intriguing, but you're scared you might bomb it. Say you're thinking of trying out for the school play, but what if you *don't* make it? Say you're thinking about submitting a poem to a magazine, but what if they reject you? Fawn says, go for it anyway!

Don't spend your entire life trying to avoid making mistakes. Some teens will worry so much about making a mistake that they just don't try. They are so afraid to fail that they don't challenge themselves. But a failure is not a measure of you as a person.

I learned from interviewing many successful women that they all failed at one time or another. But they saw it as a learning opportunity. And when one thing didn't work out for them, another thing—sometimes a better opportunity—happened instead.

Move forward. Take what you learn and say, "What's next?" It's not about where you are going as much as it is that you are going!

Sometimes we fail because we don't try enough. That *is* a failure, but it can also be a lesson for future endeavors. Sometimes we fail because we don't have what it takes to pull off a particular challenge. But don't we get points for trying? Of course we do! And don't we get points for learning something about ourselves in the process? Absolutely!

So, fail sometimes. It's so much better than never even trying.

◎ Listen to Yourself ◎

It seems as though everyone is telling you how you are supposed to act, what you should want to do, what you should wear—like they are trying to tell *you* who *you* are supposed to be. Sometimes you end up listening to everyone else, but you forget to listen to the most important person: yourself.

Susie Wang didn't forget to listen to herself. Susie owns a company, Aqua Dessa, which she started a few years ago when she was still in college. It's an all-natural beauty products line that uses no synthetic ingredients. She started the company with little money, testing her products in her boyfriend's chemistry lab. Now it's a multimillion-dollar company with a fan base from all over the world. Even celebrities use her products—and she's only 25!

But before Susie became a success, she heard a lot of negative messages when she was growing up—a whole lot.

Susie had a difficult childhood in Korea. When she was very young, she was kidnapped and then became homeless. She was sent to an orphanage for a few years, where she experienced severe abuse and neglect. Her parents finally were able to find her, and brought her to America. Here in America, she grew up poor. Susie always grew up with negative people around her. She faced severe prejudice because she was poor and Asian, and was the kid without any friends who got picked on in school. Susie remembers it this way:

> In elementary school, I faced a lot of prejudice because I was different in many ways. I was Asian so I looked different, I couldn't dress in the coolest clothes because I couldn't afford it, so I dressed differently. I thought, acted, and felt different from most of my peers. I was picked on for being myself. The teachers didn't like me, either. I had teachers who actually told me I wouldn't amount to anything. I felt worthless, like I was a second-class citizen.
>
> What made me happy was the wonderful world of beauty. Even as a child I was fascinated by cosmetics and the way they made me feel. I loved to transform myself with color. I always fantasized how wonderful it would be to be able to be the one to formulate the cosmetics that I loved so much.

How did Susie keep listening to herself, even though everyone else was telling her she was worthless, that she was wrong, that her passion didn't matter? Read her advice and find out how:

Stay true to your values. A lot of people were mean to me, and that almost made me into a mean person, too. I remember wondering why everyone was so hateful to me. In the orphanage and in my elementary school, cruelty was the way of life. But even then I knew it was better to be a nice and kind-hearted person. I refused to accept that a person needs to be cruel and step on others, even though that is what I was seeing all around me. I talked to God and prayed for strength. I did my best to stay kind even in the midst of all the meanness. And I didn't let others taint me.

Don't let others put you down. Somehow, even through the worst of my childhood, I knew that what other people said was not always true, that I should believe in myself. I knew I was worthwhile, that all the hurtful things others said about me were not true. I didn't believe them and didn't let their hate affect me. I knew in my heart I was better than people said I was. I just knew it. I knew the people putting me down had to be ignorant to make such comments. I told myself that their words had no value and no meaning. I didn't let their negativity cloud my reality of who I really was.

I also learned that the more I retaliated, the more I reacted, the more they tormented me. When I ignored them, pretended their words didn't hurt me (although they did), it wasn't fun for them so they might stop.

In an odd way, they only extended my motivation. I wanted to prove to myself and them that I was better than they said. It made me study harder, and motivated me to be a better student and an overall better person.

Find something positive that makes you feel better. Whether it's dancing, swimming, or painting, find something healthful that makes you feel good and indulge in it. When everyone told me I was ugly because I looked different from them, I made a whole escape ritual for myself. It gave me such pleasure to play with makeup and take care of myself. For me, bathing rituals were relaxing and good therapy for me. I loved to pamper myself, making facial masks out of things like crushed peaches and honey and cucumbers. And it wasn't just for my outside beauty, it was not vanity. It was for my inner self. I used to pour milk in my bathtub and soak my worries away.

Hang in there. I believe when people are faced with hardship in their life, and they can overcome them, they inherit strength. When I was a little girl, I had to overcome a great deal just to survive. I believe it made me stronger, and has helped me love and trust myself and have enough confidence to start a company in my early 20s (I'm now 25).

Despite all that, I wouldn't trade my life in for someone else's because I know it made me stronger and made me who I am today.

✳ Appreciate Yourself ✳

Kathy Buckley has not had it easy. She was molested as a child. She was labeled retarded, until it was discovered that she had a hearing loss. She was an outcast in school. One day, she lay out on the beach and a lifeguard drove over her with a jeep, putting her in and out of a wheelchair for two years. Oh, and she's had cancer, too.

I don't know any woman of any size or age that is 100 percent happy with her body. It's sad that even supermodels have complaints. Most models I work with are insecure. Their careers are based solely on their appearance.

The average size of an American woman is five foot three, 140 pounds, size 12 to 14. But what you see on TV is a size 2 and 4. It's important to get a grip on what is real compared to what is fantasy. You don't like your size? That's okay. Focus on your assets; focus on your great hair, nails, smile. Everybody has *parts* of themselves they like, so focus on those!

When you walk into a room, walk with good posture and smile—that's what people are going to see. No one notices body flaws but you. Think of people in history whose lives you admire. What do you admire about them? Very rarely will it be their body size.

So often we wait to do something, saying things like, "I'm not going to the beach until I lose 10 pounds." Don't wait! I used to live my life waiting. Do what you want to now. You'll never know what will happen!

—Katie Arons is a Ford plus-size model and the founder of the online zine *Extra Hip!*

But even after all that, Kathy, a comedian and motivational speaker, says she now realizes that there is no one she would rather be. She says:

The way you are made is the way you are supposed to be. If you see someone gorgeous walking around in her tight jeans with her belly button sticking out, it's tempting to think, "I want to be her." You need to stop thinking that way. That's the way *she* is supposed to be, not the way *you* are supposed to be.

We always want what someone else has. "I want her hair." "I want her body." In my case, it was: "Everyone has boobs but me." But when you appreciate what you have, that is what makes you beautiful. Beauty is what goes on in the inside that shines outward. The sparkle in eyes, your smile, your attitude. I've seen a lot of stereotypically beautiful women in show business, and you know what? They can't tie their own shoes. (I think that is when they came out with Velcro!) There is nothing wrong with being beautiful on the outside, but there is everything wrong if you can't find the beauty within you.

Each and every one of us was put on this earth to be an individual. The best gift you can give yourself and the universe is to become you as you. Not you as Britney. Not you compared to anyone else. You as you. Each one of us came into this world with a unique package. I wish I had known when I was younger how beautiful I really was. I missed the opportunity to enjoy being myself. I was always trying to be someone else. Everyone on this earth has something to contribute. The only real disability is a bad attitude.

◈ Have More Fun ◈

Okay, life isn't *all* fun and games. But why can't most of it be? Seriously, why not be . . . less serious.

Super Clea and Keva Marie are the authors of *Hey Day! Super Amazing, Funk-da-Crazing, Ultra-Glazing Things to Do, Make and Ponder Every Day of the Year.* They've got tons of ideas in their book about how to be, as they put it, "funner." Clea and Keva say this:

When we were teens, we were both way too serious, creatively frustrated, even a little depressed. Every little thing seemed to be a life-and-death deal. A bad thing happened, and it was like the end of the world. A bad week felt like a month . . . a bad month seemed like a year. Hey, we all have bad days and bad moods. But then we realized, as dorky as it sounds, that we could channel that energy into good. We could write and shoot photos and make clothes and sell homemade cupcakes; we could keep busy with the silly and the fun.

So, first step: Loosen up. From their book, *Hey Day!* (and from their very own mouths), here are Keva and Clea's ways to do it:

Embrace your dorkiness. There are embarassing, awkward, freaky sides to everyone. Like, you can celebrate your inner dork with an inner dork mobile. Take the dorkiest photos you have of yourself (you know, the kinds of pictures you want to rip up!) and hang them on a clothes hanger. It's a constant reminder that being a dork is fun; it's way okay!

Celebrate YOU. There's nobody like you, so celebrate your unique self. Make a photo self-portrait. Take pictures of each of your body parts, like your head, then your arm, then your tummy, then legs. Then put them all together in a photo collage.

Don't be afraid to be silly. Lose the fear of looking stupid. Find ridiculous things to do and enjoy. Get rid of your inhibitions and act crazy.

Create traditions. Not just holiday traditions, but some for any day you want to do a certain thing. Like have an Oscar party on Oscar night. Every Christmas, Clea watches *Willy Wonka and the Chocolate Factory*. On the Fourth of July, Keva gets together with pals and hangs out on her deck and tries out all the beauty tips from the teenie mags.

Find things you like and have fun with them. In our book, we have a whole page on things to do with buttons. (Hey, we like buttons!) If you like something, why shouldn't you make friends with it?

Create a Future File. When you're reading magazines, you see things you like. You soak it in, but then later on you won't have any recollection of that very thing that grabbed you. So from now on, anytime you see something in a magazine that you like, cut it out. Put it in a Future File. It's really just an elaborate way to hold on to magazine clippings and, therefore, your thoughts. Have different files on things like Fashions, Jobs, Places to Live, Books to Read. Then, say, something about Seattle catches your eye, and you stick it in the Places to Live file. And when you need inspiration, you open your file and look through everything in it and remember.

Involve your girlfriends. Get together with your friends and have fun. Have a potluck at school, where you all bring an assigned part of the meal (like Clea brings a main dish, Keva brings a dessert) to share. Play a board game, like Scrabble. Have an outdoor movie night. Put a small TV in the window facing outside. Set up lawn chairs in rows and watch the "movies"! Set up a kiddie pool in your backyard, get a beach ball, and put some beach chairs in the pool. Put on some sunscreen, drink lemonade, and gossip. Or, get out the Slip 'n Slide!

Have a happy day. Forget all your troubles and think only cheerful thoughts. Smile lots (even if you don't mean it). Hum. Play with a puppy or a kitten. Walk with a bounce. Or dare to skip. Wear yellow (it's the happiest of colors!). Draw happy faces and sunflowers in the margins of all your papers today. Go to the library. Look up Elvis and chick painters and alien space ships. Sit back and imagine yourself in an exciting situation.

These things may sound trite or, um, silly (and they are a little!), but when you learn not to take yourself too seriously, the bumps along the road (and there will be bumps—that's life!) are just a little smoother. The best part of being, in our humble opinion, is exploring new things and hanging with great friends. Cheesy? Maybe. But who cares? We're dorks and we're proud!

❖ Act Like a Princess ❖

You've read the book. You've seen the movie. Here's the scoop on how you, too, can be a Princess, by *The Princess Diaries* author herself, Meg Cabot:

> Let's face it: Wouldn't we all love to find out that we are secretly princesses, as Mia Thermopolis does in my book, *The*

F reak. Frock. Geek. Jock. This is how people got branded at my high school. Back then you fell into one of these categories, and it was tough to move up or out. I was one of the few who went from being a nerd to becoming popular. And even though I achieved this hard-to-reach goal, I still felt as though I never fit in. I realize now that as much as I wanted to blame my friends, in the end it was my problem.

To re-brand myself as cool, I faked my way to fitting in. I bought clothes I thought would impress my friends, and on the way to school made up wild stories to tell them at lunch. As a result, my senior year I was nominated biggest BS'er—proof that everyone could see right through my false image.

Great brands like Oprah and Nike are loved because they are clear, authentic, and consistent. You always know what you're going to get from them and they're always themselves.

One of life's biggest secrets is that you can succeed by just being you, too.

—Robin Fisher Roffer is president of
Big Fish Marketing, Inc., and the author of
*Make a Name For Yourself—
8 Steps Every Woman Needs to Create a
Personal Brand Strategy for Success.*

Princess Diaries? Sadly, there aren't enough countries on the planet for each one of us to get a chance to reign supreme. Still, it's possible at least to act like a princess, even if you can't really *be* one. Follow the guidelines listed below, and you just might get mistaken for royalty someday:

Be kind. There is an old saying that says it is easier to catch flies with honey than with vinegar. Princesses understand this, and that's why they are sweet to everyone—even those who deserve less than regal treatment. Remember, nothing confuses an enemy more than kindness . . . or puts her more off her guard. Princesses are never purposefully rude or mean . . . at least to anyone's face. And random acts of kindness—Instant Messaging someone who seems down; offering to go to the movies with the class loser; letting your best friend borrow your new denim mini—will earn you big-time points in Princess Heaven. And you never know when someday you might be in a position where you need someone to return the favor!

> Say what you mean and mean what you say.
>
> —Jessica, 18, California

Be assertive. Just because you're kind does not mean you have to be a pushover. Don't let other people tell you what to do, particularly when you feel what they are proposing is morally or legally wrong. That doesn't mean you have free license to be rude to them, however. Always state your mind sweetly, but firmly. If that fails to sway people to your way of thinking, simply do whatever you have to do in order to extract yourself from the situation. Then do exactly what you intended to do in the first place—just do it politely. And remember, it is princess-like to be assertive; it is unprincess-like to purposefully hurt yourself or others—except in self-defense, of course.

Be happy. Sure, you feel down in the dumps sometimes. Who doesn't? But a princess always puts her best face forward. So you've got a huge zit, a D in geometry, and your boyfriend was spotted at a party last night with some other girl. Never let them see that any of it is bothering you. They will marvel at your self-confidence and *joie de vivre*. People are naturally drawn to those with a ready smile and quick laugh. But don't be fake. Just concentrate on what's good in your life, not the bad stuff. Thankfully, for some reason acting like you're happy tends to make you *feel* happy, so it shouldn't be too tough, after a little practice. And it's a win-win situation: Even your parents will be astounded by your newfound lack of surliness, and that can lead to increases in allowance and extensions of curfew—more things to be happy about!

Be gracious. You can't win them all. When they lose, princesses don't let anyone know it bothers them. Sweetly congratulate the winner, then go home and pour out all those feelings of hatred and jealousy in your diary. If they never know how much it meant to you, they won't feel sorry for you when you don't get it. No princess wants anyone's pity.

And most importantly:

Be yourself. Princesses set their own trends; they do not follow the dictates of others. Can a girl with green hair wear sneakers and really be a princess? Absolutely, if she selected those accessories because she wanted them, and not just because everyone else in her class was wearing them. Can a princess play hockey? If she's doing it because she loves the sport, not because getting on the team will impress a boy, she can.

Remember, being a princess is about how you act, not who your parents are, what kind of SAT scores you got, what car you drive, or how you look—though cleanliness is next to godliness for princesses as well as the rest of the populace. Try, at least, to keep yourself—and your room—in a tidy and orderly state. Can princesses have blackheads? Of course. But they make an effort to rid themselves of such blemishes. Can princesses wear all black? Yes, but nothing ill-fitting, please. Can princesses have messy rooms? Yes, but for God's sake, there is a difference between messy and unhygienic. There is nothing princess-like about vermin.

Being yourself means being the best self you can be—exercise, eat right, and follow the dictums above. Soon your friends, not to mention the rest of the world, will be wondering just how it is that you manage to project so regal—and yet welcoming—an image.

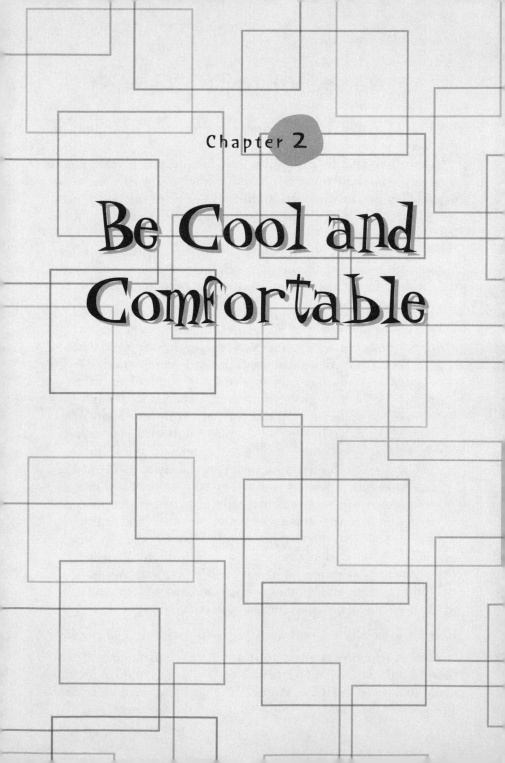

Chapter 2

Be Cool and Comfortable

❖ Make Fashion Your Slave ❖

We all have to wear clothes. Some of us just have more fun with that fact than others.

Okay, first things first. Nobody is forcing you to care about fashion if you really don't want to. But after you read what Brandon Holley has to say, you might realize you're missing out on some fun. (And if you already looove fashion, well, you're going to looove this section.)

Brandon is the editor-in-chief of *ELLEgirl* magazine, a teen fashion and beauty magazine that "celebrates an independent attitude with an international flair." Here's what Brandon says:

> Don't be a slave to fashion. Instead, make fashion *your* slave. Our philosophy at *ELLEgirl* is to get up each day and dress yourself in a way that expresses *You* on that given day.
>
> People sometimes dismiss fashion as unimportant. But fashion is not shallow, not superficial—if you look at it the right way. Fashion gives you a great opportunity for freedom of self-expression. Autonomy starts with your mind, of course. But it can be very much reflected in what you wear. When you dress independently, you tend to think independently. You develop your own personal style.
>
> Style isn't just what you put on your body. Fashion is what you wear; style is what you emanate. Style is more than simply your clothing, but it also consists of the conversations you have, the way you conduct yourself, the way you move. Audrey Hepburn was so much more than her Givenchy wardrobe; she had true style. The way you walk through your high school with your head up, shoulders back—that will be what clinches *your* style.

Here are some of Brandon's ways to have fun with your style:

Dress to express your mood. Check your mood and then dress to reflect how you feel. Maybe today you feel Marilyn Monroe glam. Tomorrow you'll feel Vintage. The next day you'll be Peasant. Just get into the mood, get into character and dress the part.

Don't be a fashion lemming. If everyone else is carrying around the same bag, carry a different one. Don't feel you have to dress like the in-crowd if you don't feel like it. Be your own person, and don't feel pressured to conform. I just got together with some of my friends from high school. We were the girls who dressed, well, *different* from everyone else in school. Although we took great pride in how we looked, we didn't bend to the trends. And now, we're all very successful in what we do and lead creative, interesting lives. We are not like some of our classmates who always went along with the crowd, who are now still part of the crowd in boring jobs. This was the path my friends and I all discovered that we took in life—still one of being independent and interesting.

Experiment with fashion. When you're a teen, fashion is your oyster. All opportunities are open to you now to try new things with your hair, your clothes. You'll make some fashion mistakes, but that's fine; at least you tried. You aren't supposed to just wake up one day and know your perfect style.

Mix it up. Style doesn't mean buying only clothes with labels or designer brands. It might be a jacket from your dad's closet and your grandmother's brooch, paired with a button-down white shirt and jeans. Girls with style today are mixing it up, wearing DKNY pants with a shirt from a vintage store that cost $2. They're wearing their dad's button-down shirts, his tie as a belt, their own jeans—and looking great!

Be
Yourself!!!
—Laura, 16, Ohio

Be inspired by fashion. I'm a fashion-magazine junkie. But there are other ways I get inspired as well. Here are some of them:

- *Watch fashion shows for fun and for ideas.* I like to go to fashion shows of my favorite designers, like Marc by Marc Jacobs. It doesn't change my life, but it's fun and exhilarating to be in this creative environment. There is an enormous amount of artistic expression and there's so much buzz surrounding the event.

  But you don't have to actually go to a fashion show to have fun with them. You can read about them in magazines and online.

And you can look at more than the clothes and the trends. I admire the creativity and individuality in the shows and the photography. I love to see how the different photographers take pictures of the same model walking down the runway, and then interpret it so that each ends up telling a different story.

- *Look to the past.* This idea is from Jennifur Brandt, one of our contributors. Go to the library and check out fashion books from different eras. Grab what appeals to you, say, some sixties new wave French books. Xerox the pages you find inspiring. And buy some old magazines from the sixties and seventies from a used bookstore (you also can get them on eBay, but they tend to be expensive there). Look through them for style inspiration.

- *Make an Inspiration Board.* I have my fashion editors make an Inspiration Board before every shoot. Here's a way you can adapt it for yourself. You're going to pretend you're a fashion stylist. Go into your closet and, say you have twenty items, pull them out. Then raid your mom's closet (with permission, *of course*) and your dad's, for things like a tie you like, button-down shirts, and big jackets. Now . . .

1. Lay out all the clothes around you in your room.

2. Put the pieces together to make different outfits.

3. Experiment with different looks.

4. Take a Polaroid or a regular photo of each outfit.

5. Hang all the pictures on the inside of your closet door, on your wall, on your bulletin board.

6. Label the photos according to what mood or look they seem to fit.

7. On the days you don't know what you want to wear, or feel uninspired, you can look at your Inspiration Board and say, "Oh! That's today!"

You can even take it a step further and put up pictures of not just clothing, but anything that inspires you—record covers, celebrities, . . . hey it could be pictures of Gandhi. Whatever inspires you!

Learn to Accept a Compliment

"Thank you" are the only two words you need to know and use when someone says, "You look so great today!" No lengthy explanations to minimize your brilliant taste are required. Control yourself. "Thank you" honors you and honors the good taste of the person who complimented you. Don't spoil the moment with elaborate details about garage sales, hand-me-downs, clearance sales, blah, blah, blah, blah, blah. You look great. Face it. Accept it. Say, "Thank you." That's it.

—Courtesy of Brenda Kinsel, author of *In the Dressing Room with Brenda.*

• *Get your friends in on it.* Sleep over at a friend's house and put together an outfit of her clothes for you to wear. Then hit your closet for her wardrobe. Wear your "new" outfits to school. (A random funny thing to do is to go into the girl's bathroom and trade outfits with your friend. Then walk out and pretend like nothing happened and everything's totally normal. See if anyone notices!) Get together with your friends for a photo shoot. Take pictures of yourselves in different fashions.

Spot Trends

I grew up a few hours north of New York City. We were about a year behind the city girls in trends, though. Then I started going to camp near the city and seeing all these girls in the latest and greatest. So I brought the trends home with me. I literally bought, bartered, and begged the clothes off the other campers' backs.

Some were fashion hits, like the graffiti jeans. Some were major misses, like the sneakers with giant salamanders on them. (And I did all that girl's kitchen duty for a week to get them! What was I thinking?!)

But hey, I was just an *amateur* trendspotter. Isabel González is a pro at it. As the "Trendspotting" editor for *Teen People* magazine, Isabel is responsible for staying in touch with 10,000 *Teen People* Trendspotters. She tells us this:

> Our Trendspotters are teens from around the world who give me guidance as to what is happening on the street level and in their hoods. From their favorite new jeans, to the music that they just have to listen to, these 10,000 teens tell me what's hot and what's not.
>
> I also do a lot of trendspotting myself. In addition to these teens clueing me in, a lot of times I already have a clue about what's breaking through the pop culture psyche. The best way I can explain this is that it's part intuitive (you just know when something looks hot and fresh and when something absolutely doesn't) and part learned (see the 3 Rules of Trendspotting that follow). If you master the learning part, eventually it *all* becomes intuitive.

Here are Isabel's three rules:

Rule 1: What goes around comes around in due time, and about 20 percent different than before.

Sometimes you just know what is hot and what isn't. Cool things scream out at you, like the recent resurrection of off-the-shoulder bohemian 1970s blouses; I just knew that trend was going to blow up. When something has gone away for a while and makes a new appearance, there's something fresh about it. Of course, it's got to be gone for the right amount of time. For example, it's not time yet to see guys wearing Don Johnson *Miami Vice* pastel suits, but in time they might make an appearance anew. Fortunately though, a lot of times it's not like the original trend is reborn exactly how it once was.

Take bell bottoms for example. They reemerged on the scene a few years ago, but something was different about them. First off, they weren't as outrageously wide (think flare jeans), the pockets sat lower on the butt, they came in darker denim, and they were made of stiffer jean material. It's like when a trend comes back from the past, part of what determines whether it is cool or not is how it's reinvented and re-created. There usually has to be a new twist on the look (the 20 percent change rule).

Rule 2: Find the trendsetters and check out what they are wearing.

One of the best ways to spot trends is by just watching people. I have always loved to go to parties, but half the fun is just checking out everyone's looks. When you watch people you always can group them into a few style categories, from the prepsters to the goths to the punks to the trendies. Each style group (and those who embrace bits of all styles) is unique and different, not better or worse. Usually I take cues from the folks who dress differently from the rest of the pack. These people are edgier, more daring, and more creative with the way that they dress. They are the kids who first wore tube socks as arm cuffs, only to have that look later embraced by Britney Spears. These are usually the people who set trends. No matter how weird it may look at first glance, no doubt they are starting something that will set the pace for others to follow. I'll never forget how when I was a freshman in high school I loved to cuff up my super-long jeans for a 1950s retro look. Low and behold, a few years later (I wish it had taken less time than that, but better late than never) cuffed jeans became all the rage in my neck of the woods.

Rule 3: Read international magazines and travel as much as possible.

Magazines are a great source of trends. I'm always poring over all the international magazines—and not just the glossy European ones. I study all the international magazines because there is always something fresh and new going on somewhere in the world, and a lot of times a trend starts somewhere else and slowly makes its way stateside.

Courage is the ability to do anything but blend in.

—Whitney, 17, Ohio

I went to Madrid, and all these girls were wearing chandelier earrings from Morocco and Egypt, and I was thinking, "That is so cool!" Then the supermodel Gisele was spotted wearing a pair at a Lakers game a few months later, and boom—it's now a certified trend. Move over, big gold hoops; hello ethnic jewelry! If you can't get your hands on international mags, *Teen People* is a great resource because we report on trends—like the earrings we spotted in Spain—before anybody else does!

✦ Know What Looks Good on You ✦

Has this happened to you? Your friend who comes to school one day and just looks WOW! in her new shirt and pants. You ask her where she got her outfit, and you run to the store to get yourself that outfit, too. And you put them on and . . . there's no wow. You don't even look like you're wearing the same clothes. You look okay, but just not great. What happened?

Leah Feldon is a style consultant who wrote a bestselling book called *Does This Make Me Look Fat?* She gives the answers to how to wear clothes that look good on *you*. Not just good-looking clothes, but clothes for *you*. Here's what she has to say:

The teen years are years to experiment to see what styles are most you. And they are also the years where you can wear all of the trends and actually get away with it. You can experiment with style.

But you need to pay a lot of attention to your body. So how can you wear what's in style without sacrificing what looks good on you? You need to adapt the trend to your own body. Keep your goals in mind: (1) to look as good as *you* possibly can, and (2) to feel comfortable with your personal style.

Here's how Leah says to do it:

Do a personal physical inventory. Before you shop, you need to get a handle on the real you. Look in the mirror. The goal is to do an objective review of yourself. Don't be tough on yourself! Don't say, "I look fat!" or "I hate my chest!" Look at your reflection and pretend it is a loving friend you are trying to help. Pretend you want to give this "friend" really good advice.

Ask yourself: What are this friend's best features? What does she really like? What are this friend's challenges in her appearance? What would be better to not notice as much?

Evaluate the trends—for YOU. Look at a trend you want to wear. Suppose you like low-rise jeans. Ask yourself: "What will they do to my body?" They have a horizontal line that splits your body right at the hips. So, are your hips an area you want to highlight?

Play up your good points. Accentuate the positives. Which parts of your body did you identify that you liked the best? You want people to notice these parts most.

Check out some clothing trends and consider if they are right for you . . . or if you should skip 'em. Leah gives her advice:

- *Cropped tops:* Cute look. But if your midsection isn't your best feature, try wearing a short top over a longer one. You'll get the cropped top look without exposing your midriff.

- *Tank tops:* A classic. Anybody can wear them. If you're very big busted, think about wearing two tank tops together for a little extra support. They can be the same color or a different color. Let a little of the second color peak out for style interest.

- *Capris:* Can be a tough proportion to work with. Generally they're not that flattering, especially if you're short. If they don't look quite right on you, go for a cropped pant—hemmed any-where from right below the bottom of the calf to just above the ankle. This will give you same feel as a capri but a more flatter-ing line.

- *Flares:* Since flare pants are usually pretty tight through the thighs, they look best on girls with long skinny legs—which doesn't mean you can't wear them if you're not a model. Just make sure the pants aren't *too* tight through the thighs, and that the flare bottoms are not ultra-wide.

- *Mini skirts:* Can look cute depending on what you wear with them. Usually best with low heels; high heels and minis can look a bit tarty. If your legs are not your best point, opt for slightly longer lengths.

- *Long skirts:* Everybody can wear them. The best long skirts are not stiff, but move with the body a bit. For daytime, long skirts are usually best no longer than ankle length.

- *A-line flare skirts:* A good choice if you have ample hips.

- *Peasant tops:* Technically anybody can wear them. Whether or not you opt to is more a matter of personality. If you're more of a tailored or tomboy type, you probably won't feel as comfortable in them as a friend who's more girly.

- *Ruffles:* Just don't overdo them. Keep ruffles small and minimal, and you can't go wrong.

- *Off one shoulder:* This kind of asymmetrical neckline can look great; just make sure you've got the right kind of undergarments in your drawer—like some kind of strapless bra.

- *Tight spandex shirts:* Not a great idea if you're big-busted since they will bring attention to your breasts. Remember, you want people to notice *you* first, not your body parts. Loosen up.

You'll know it when you feel it. You'll walk over to that mirror and just feel great. So . . . comfy yet? Feeling good? Looking good!

◎ Look Model Perfect ◎ (Hint: You Already Do)

Since we're talking about fashion and style, you might be inspired to pick up some fashion magazines. You're flipping through them, and . . . wait: No whining about how you look compared to the models, remember? Here's a refresher from Jennifer Walsh, who

You and Your Bra

Did you know that 8 out of 10 women are wearing the wrong bra size? Most bra experts suggest getting fitted for a bra at least once a year, since gaining or losing weight, or even working out, can completely change your shape and bra size.

Here's a quick guide to finding the perfect bra to fit your dynamic duo, courtesy of Rachel Weingarten of PlanetPretty.com.

Measure Up

- Stand up straight, and relax.

- Use a soft measuring tape to measure all the way around your body. Place the tape measure right underneath your breasts. Add 5 to whatever your measurement is, so if your measurement is 27 inches, add 5 to that number, and you'll come up with 32 (round up to the next even number if you come up with an odd number). Cool— you've just figured out your *band size.*

- Next it's time to figure out your *cup size.* While you're wearing a bra, measure the fullest part of your chest (across the nipple) without stretching the tape too tight. If you need to, enlist a friend to help you to get the tape measure around your entire back. We'll choose 35 as an example.

- Subtract the number from your band size (35 − 32 = 3). Voila, now you've got your band and cup sizes, so based on the following guide: 0=AA, 1=A, 2=B, 3=C, 4=D, 5=DD, 6=DDD, our sample bra is a 32B.

Okay, so now you know what size bra you wear, but how do you know if your bra fits right?

(continues)

Fit In

- While putting on your bra, bend over and let your breasts fall naturally into the cups.

- The center of your bra should lie flat against your breastbone; it shouldn't gap at all.

- Make sure that the bra cups are smooth, with no wrinkles. (If it looks all wrinkly, it doesn't need to be ironed; it's most probably too big for you.)

- Adjust the straps to make sure that they're the right length and comfort level.

- Turn to the side and look in a mirror to see whether the back of your bra rides up. If it does, then the bra doesn't fit correctly. The back of your bra should rest comfortably against the middle of your back.

Look Good!

- Before you buy any bra, you might want to try it on underneath your clothes, to see if it gives you the look and shape that you're most comfortable with.

- When you're wearing a bra under sheer clothes, your best bet is a bra that matches your skin tone—not the top that you'll be wearing.

started her career as a model. She's still involved in the beauty and fashion scene, now as president and editor-in-chief of The Beauty Bar and thebeautybar.com. Here's what Jennifer has to say:

Before a model starts working with the photographer, she can spend up to an hour or so with the hair stylist. Then she'll spend at least an hour with the makeup artist. A professional wardrobe stylist picks out the clothes (and usually has a lot of adjusting to do). A lighting technician or two may be used to make sure the best light is utilized on the

How do people usually judge beauty? Well, that's an easy one. People usually judge others by what they can see: face, clothes, hair, makeup, and especially the shape of the body. Outside things can be easily noticed, while what a person is like on the inside takes time to be seen. Sometimes people can be more beautiful on the outside than on the inside, but Inner Beauty is what really counts.

It can be hard to turn beauty inside out because it's so much easier to make quick judgments based on appearance. Discovering inner beauty takes time. People should be judged on their inner beauty, where their true characteristics are. Your outside appearance is just a cover over the real, true person inside. So don't pay any attention to outer beauty, but focus on Inner Beauty instead. Pay attention to signs of Inner Beauty. Notice when people are brave, helpful, loving, sharing, expressive, artistic, and thoughtful.

Don't be afraid to let your Inner Beauty shine out and to show the world who you really are!

—Alyssa Gellatly, 12. Alyssa has been on the Girls Editorial Board of *New Moon* magazine for two years. *New Moon* has a new campaign called Turn Beauty Inside Out at www.newmoon.org.

model. Then the photographer works with her. Through all this, there is usually a producer on the set to supervise.

While the model is posing for the pictures, all of the above people are looking on to make sure that nothing is out of place, and that everything looks as perfect as it can. Depending on what kind of shoot it is, there can be a lot of pulling and primping on the set.

Then the models pose and the photographers shoot.

You might think this is all that happens, but it's not. Computers and technology allow for some extreme altering of pictures. If the client (the person needing this specific shot) doesn't think the white of the model's eyes are white enough, the computer graphic department can whiten them. Her lines and wrinkles are literally erased with the click of a button. Blemishes are erased. The model's body can literally be elongated to make her seem taller. Her bust line can be enhanced to better fill out a blouse. Have you ever noticed that some celebrities seem to have larger breasts in print than when they are on TV? It is all computer generated!

So think of that next time you start to feel inferior because that model is so perfect . . . Remember what it took to get her that way!

> No one can tell you how to be yourself. Only YOU are YOU! Don't worry about what other people think. If Aisha doesn't like your dress, so what? She's not you. Is Ethan giving you a hard time about your nose? Hey, that sort of thing is what makes you YOU!
>
> —Cecily, 14, California

◉ Dress Right ◉ for a Job Interview

You want the job. You think you've got what it takes. But do you look like you do?

Sherry Maysonave, author of *Casual Power* and president of Empowerment Enterprises says that how you present yourself in any interview is often the determining factor in whether or not you get the job!

It seems as though it should be your skills, your talents, your experience that lands you the job. But all those things can be quickly forgotten if you walk in the door dressed inappropriately. And is that a good reason to lose out on a job? I don't think so.

Here are the Dos and Don'ts from Sherry:

DO WEAR:

Office Job Interview

Daytime dress, dressier than
   school clothes

Skirts, long or short (but not too
   short), preferably with stockings

Tops, long or short sleeves with a
   conservative neckline

Stylish shoes

Tastefully applied makeup

Jewelry, simple

(If you have a business suit or
   blazer, this would be a good
   place to wear it.)

Fast Food Restaurant Interview

Pants, but not jeans

Skirts, long or short

Tops, long or short sleeves with
   a conservative neckline

Sneakers (clean) or stylish shoes

Tastefully applied makeup

Jewelry, simple

(Clean hands and nails are
   essential for any food-
   handling job. Really long hair
   will not bode well for food
   handlers either. If your hair is
   ultra-long, pull it back or put
   it up.)

DON'T WEAR TO ANY JOB INTERVIEW:

Mini skirts

Sandals

Perfume

Weird hairstyles

Large banana clips in your hair

Body piercings that show

Little-girl styles

Workout attire

Leather pants

Tank tops, halter tops, T-shirts

Overdone makeup (such as
   black lipstick)

Bright or unusual nail polish

Funky hair colors

Tattoos that show

Jeans or shorts

Sweat shirts or sweat pants

Short leather skirts

Rings on every finger or lots of
   bracelets

✖ Wear Makeup to Flatter, ✖ Not Frighten

You've seen them: The girl whose blush is in bright red circles on
her cheeks, making her look like she's auditioning to be a clown in

the circus. The girl whose foundation leaves an orange rim on her neck. The girl who has so much makeup on that it looks like she's wearing a mask.

Hey, it's fun to experiment with different looks, and some girls get pretty artistic with their makeup. But most girls do best with a more natural look, using makeup to enhance their looks.

Joan Tinnell owns a spa called Spahhs that has a makeup studio where she offers courses for teens on how to apply makeup.

Joan says girls fall into two stages with regard to makeup:

Stage 1: Starting out

This is the stage when your parents first let you wear makeup—or you usually don't wear it, but might want a little for a special occasion. Your goal is to look fresh and to enhance your features.

- Use softer earth or pink tones to look great without looking "too much."

- Wear lip gloss with a pale pink or peach sheen.

- You might try clear mascara to separate lashes. You also can use it to comb unruly eyebrows.

- Avoid skin makeup. If you break out, a little concealer would be fine.

Stage 2: The next level

Stage 2 is for when you're an older teen and you've been through Stage 1 for a while. It's also good for special occasions. Be careful not to overdo it. When girls use too much makeup, they look like they don't know what they're doing.

- Don't use liquid foundation. Try lightly using dusting powder or a dual foundation/powder.

- Use a little blush. Make sure it blends in so you don't look phony.

- Try lipsticks in bolder shades.

- Mascara is best in black/brown. Pure black can be harsh. Blue and purple look too fake.

- Don't use liquid eyeliner. If you want to use liner, use powder.

◇ Zap Your Zits ◇

Erin Jacobsen is an esthetician for Ole Hendrikson Face/Body Spa in L.A., a popular place for models and celebrities who have cameras close up on their skin. Here are her suggestions:

Cleanse. If you have acne, use a good cleanser made for normal/oily skin. Be careful not to overcleanse, or the natural oxygenation process will not be able to take place, leaving your skin crusty, red, and irritated. To kill bacteria, take a teaspoon of tea tree oil and pour it into a sink of warm, not hot, water. Soak a towel in it, wring out the towel, and place it on your face for a few minutes. This will heal the skin tissue. It might make your face a little red for a bit. Do this three times a week.

> **Compliment other people. It makes them feel good and you feel good, too.**
> —Carrie, 14, Nebraska

Use a toner. A toner will help take the shine away and make your skin look less greasy. You can make a toner at home by filling a 4-ounce bottle with 1 ounce of distilled water and then filling it with half lemon juice and half apple juice. Pour a little bit on two cotton pads and rub it on your face. The mixture of citric acid, malic acid, and water works wonders to calm the skin and help in the cell-renewal process.

Consider moisturizing. Moisturizer can be used on oily or acne-prone skin if it is non-comedogenic, which means it won't clog pores.

Drink lots of water. Water will cleanse your body and flush out your system.

Eat a nutritious diet. An unbalanced diet, or one with too much sugar, can contribute to acne.

Sleep and relax. Get a good night's sleep (see page 13) and try not to stress out too much. Not enough rest and too much stress can contribute to acne.

These suggestions will help with the start of mild acne. For serious acne, you should consult a dermatologist. And be patient—acne doesn't often go away overnight.

☼ Look Great in a Photo ☼

School photos. Family photo albums. Picture booths. Photos on little stickers. Photo ops are *everywhere.*

Celebrity makeup artist Rachel Weingarten has gotten many a face ready for a photo. This is what she has to say: "Did you ever notice how some people always come out perfect in pictures? These chicas aren't always the most traditionally beautiful, but they do know how to pose and which looks are the most flattering."

Try these picture-taking tips from one of Rachel's Web sites, PlanetPretty.com, for a picture perfect look. (If you don't wear makeup yet, no prob. Just skip that advice and be a natural beauty.)

Don't go to extremes. If you're going to be photographed at a special occasion like your prom or your older sister's wedding, don't use this time to break out the funky new makeup tricks that you've read about. Practice your makeup look several times before the event, and even get all dressed up and have a friend photograph you, so you can have a better idea of what you'll look like in print.

Your prom or sister's wedding is not the time to turn your brown eyes blue with colored contacts, or to dye your mousy brown hair platinum blonde. You may end up hating the effect, and having to live with the proof in picture form forever!

Easy on the foundation. Forget the old rule of using foundation on your entire face—unless your skin is really blotchy and uneven. You'll find that applying the right concealer—using a tapered concealer brush—can cover up a multitude of sins. Always start with less (you can layer some more on afterwards!). Some places to lighten up are the inner and outer corners of your eyes, right around and underneath your nostrils, and the outer corner of your lips.

Cover up your zits. Use a concealer that matches your skin tone and dab a drop on at a time, then follow with translucent powder to set. (If you're plagued by acne or persistent pimples, it's time to visit a dermatologist, who can prescribe cleansers or medication to help you with your spotty skin.)

Make your eyes stand out. A drop of white or baby blue frosty eye shadow blended right under the arch of your eyebrow really opens up your eyes. (You might also want to try a dab in the inner corner of your eyes.) To make your eyes really pop in photos, line only your top eyelid, and use mascara on the top lashes only. Eyes that are lined on top and bottom tend to look smaller in pictures.

Prevent a washed-out look. If you're fair, and you want to avoid looking washed out, apply some cream blush to the apples of your cheeks, and try darkening blond brows with a bit of a darker shadow with ash tones in it.

Blend. Whatever you do or try, blend, blend, and then blend some more! Well-blended makeup shows up beautifully in pictures.

Even out your pores. Translucent powder applied with a big fluffy brush helps to even out your pores, and to give your face a more uniform look. It also minimizes shine, and flash photos tend to magnify shine on your T-zone (forehead, nose, and chin).

Set your makeup. Spritz some Evian water (you know, those spray cans that you see in the drugstore) all over your face. Be careful not to scrunch up your face, or you'll leave yourself with lines of makeup where they shouldn't be.

Do your hair first! If you can, do your hair before your makeup. Hot blow dryers and hairspray can destroy your carefully applied makeup!

Hints for glasses wearers. If you wear glasses, don't over-apply your makeup since it will be magnified by the lens. Consider taking off your glasses for photos, or move your chin down slightly so lenses don't catch a glare.

Try to find your best angle. Or, try to look up at the camera with your neck stretched. (If you pay attention to pictures of your favorite celebs, you'll notice that they usually pose the same way in pictures.)

Pose. Try tilting your head slightly. This emphasizes your bone structure, and you'll look relaxed and friendly.

SMILE! *Truly* beautiful girls aren't always the ones with perfect hair, teeth, or skin. Truly beautiful girls realize that all the beauty tips and makeup in the world can't make someone with a bad attitude and a scowl look beautiful! The right makeup and clothes might help you to look better in a picture, but to be a real beauty, you just *need to let your inner beauty and gorgeous self shine through!*

Say cheese!

❧ Throw a Party ❧

Your BFF's surprise birthday party! The killer after-prom bash! An anti–Valentine's Day party for your single friends!

It's party time!

Throwing a fabulous party is a skill that can boost your rep and make you an entertaining superstar. Lisa Serantes plans parties for the Express clothing stores. Here are some of her party tips:

1. **Music, music, music!** I can't emphasize the importance of having great music (and, ideally, a decent sound system to play it on). Consider your guests when deciding what your playlist will be; a good way to make sure everyone hears a few fave tunes is to ask each guest to bring a CD. Don't play it too loud at first; let everyone mingle and talk with each other first. As the night goes on, you can turn up the volume.

2. **Focus on food.** Food is a great way to get your guests to say, "Yeah, that was a good party!" Provide the favorites and even try a few new recipes, if you dare. Remember: Presentation is everything! Don't just throw the bag of chips down on a table;

put them in a cool bowl. In fact, if you really want to make a splash, paint your own serving bowls at your local pottery painting joint. Use bold colors and cool designs to paint your bowls, and make sure you tell everyone at the party about it!

3. **Dim the lights for atmosphere.** If safety allows it, scatter lighted candles around, too.

4. **Make sure to have extra toilet paper in the bathrooms.** Yeah, a bizarre detail, but you don't want an empty tube to be the most memorable thing about your bash!

5. **Capture those photo ops!** Keep a Polaroid I-Zone (you know, it makes those tiny photo stickers) or camera handy and give the instant pics to your guests. Or download photos from your digital and e-mail to all your pals! And to show all your friends who couldn't make it: "Sorry, you missed the fun!"

My friend always carries a camera to freeze the times she's having fun with the people she loves.
—Harmony, 17, Pennsylvania

Chapter 3

Be Capable

☼ Achieve a Goal ☼

What an awesome feeling when you can say, "I DID IT!"

Achieving a goal is a very empowering experience. My goal has pretty much always been to be a bestselling author of a book that helps empower and motivate girls. (So hey, um, feel free to tell your friends to buy this book! I have a goal to reach here, you know.)

Candace Hammond, a personal coach who helps teens reach their goals, offers these steps to go out and do it:

Choose a meaningful goal. You are more likely to achieve a goal if it is important to you. What's something that lights you up inside? Something you really want to do . . . making a sports team, acing a test, getting into a certain college, traveling abroad. . . . It should be positive and healthy for you.

Suppose you have a goal to accomplish, something that doesn't really spark you—like, you're not into your Spanish class, but a good grade will enable you to stay on the sports team. Work at seeing what *you* can get out of it, even if it's not your favorite thing. Maybe you're sick of practicing piano, but you have to keep taking lessons and play in a recital. Make it as rewarding as you can. For example, you might get some sheet music for a song *you* like and learn that along with what your teacher assigns. No knowledge is ever a waste. Try to see the big picture, and you can almost always find something worthwhile to help you hang in there.

Break the goal into smaller steps. A goal can look so huge when you start. So break it down into bite-size pieces, or mini-goals. It will seem more manageable. And you will have a feeling of success each time you accomplish one of the mini-goals.

Have someone to support you. It helps to be accountable to someone else. Choose a person to support you who:

- Believes in you and your goal
- Is honest
- Is supporting you for all the right reasons (it is not about *him or her;* it is about *you*)

- If possible, has some experience with what you are going through

You might choose a mentor, a teacher, a parent, or someone else you can talk to. Being accountable to a friend could be sticky. It's hard for a friend to stand up to you when you go off track. You don't need someone who will be on you so much that you can't stand it, but on the other hand sometimes those who love us can let us off too easily! Choose carefully.

> Never give up on your goals.
>
> —Megan, 13, Ohio

Move into action. Start on your plan. Touch base with yourself on a regular basis to see how you are doing.

Keep your eye on the prize. Be clear about what it is you are working toward. If you don't know what the end result will be, it will be hard to stick with it. If you want to make sure you stick with that running program so you can make the basketball team, picture yourself out on the court outrunning everyone else!

Reward yourself. Set up a reward system for yourself at various points in the process. When you've stuck with your goal for two weeks, a month, whatever works for you, do something nice for yourself. Got the grade you were working toward on that test? Treat yourself to something that would be special for you. To stick with something long term, you have to have fun!

Celebrate your successes. When you reach your goal, and of course when you achieve your mini-goals along the way, celebrate! Too often we just say, "Yeah, yeah, I did it . . . what's next?" Take the time to feel really good about what you accomplished.

❧ Bond with Your Car ❧

Let's say you've got your own car. Or you're borrowing someone else's car. Or, hey, you don't even have your license yet. You're just dreaming about cruising on the open road someday. Keep reading and prepare for the not-so-distant future.

When she was 22, Carolyn Mackler, the author of *Love and Other Four-Letter Words,* drove cross-country by herself in a green Toyota named Egg. One of the best things about her trip, she says, is that she totally bonded with her car.

Why car bonding? "Cars equal independence," says Carolyn. "You can zip off by yourself. A car *literally* takes you where you want to go. Bonding with your car can be an incredibly empowering experience."

Are you ready for a new, improved relationship with your automobile? It doesn't even have to be your *own* car. It can be borrowed from your parents or anything you happen to be driving at the moment. Hey, it doesn't even have to be a car! It can be a Jeep, an SUV, a truck. Here's Carolyn's advice on how to bond with your vehicle:

Compile a collection of driving tunes. Make mix tapes or burn CDs and stash them in the glove compartment. Roll the windows down, yodel at the top of your lungs, do car dances. Have an assortment of road mixes: sunny-day mix, rainy-day mix, highway mix, driving-alone mix.

Name your car. Even if you're only in possession of it for a few hours, naming your car is a bonding must. Here's how it goes: Think really hard about your car and then grab whatever name first pops into your head. I once rented a car for the weekend and, using this method, named it "Pooper"!

Honor the Munchie Goddess. Car food is key—crunchy, munchie, sweet, savory. Pull over to the side of the road for a quick snack. My favorite meals on wheels are caramel popcorn, Ritz Bits, strawberries, and Cinnaburst gum.

Be a good driver. Take pride in being highly capable behind the wheel. Parallel-park like butter. Learn to drive a stick shift. Know how to tackle icy patches and hairpin turns.

> Believe in yourself and believe that you can succeed in anything if you put your heart and mind into it.
> —Marianna, 17, New York

Decorate your car. Hang trinkets from the rearview mirror, pull groovy T-shirts over the seats, and tape pictures of your friends to the dashboard. If you're not driving your own car, go the more low-key route, like stashing wildflowers on the dashboard.

Be a motorhead. Pump your own gas. Know how to check your oil. Be able to walk into a mechanic's garage and say, "I need a new muffler," or "I'd like my timing belt changed."

As you become one with your vehicle, you'll quickly learn that Fred Flintstone isn't the *only* person whose feet are planted firmly on the ground while driving. In other words, bonding with your car actually helps you bond with yourself—making you confident, competent, and in control of your life (not to mention the road!).

❀ Love Math ❀

Math. ACKKKKKKKKKKKKKKKKKKKKKKKK!

That one word still strikes a moment of fear in my heart.

Math just wasn't my thing in school. It wasn't the whole "Math is for guys and not girls" thing either. I'm just naturally a writer, a words person. My favorite subjects were English and more English. Confession time. Due to a computer glitch in high school, I wasn't given math on my eleventh-grade schedule. I had an extra study hall. Hmmm. Nobody was noticing, so I just continued on, la-la-la, hoping nobody would snag me.

Then senior year. You're not going to believe this. My schedule *again* shows up with no math. And my guidance counselor never caught it. That was a lot of math I missed. Of course, I was ecstatic to be living a math-free existence.

But looking back . . . yeah, yeah. I should have taken math. (I also should have pointed out the computer glitch. Oh, the guilt!) Really, I've had a lot of catching up to do. Even a writer needs to work the numbers.

Where was Rachel Muir when I needed her? Rachel's going to tell you how you can learn to love math. She was 26 when—determined to empower girls in math, science, and technology—she launched her own business with $500 and a credit card. Now her organization is going strong; she even won an Oprah's Use Your Life Award.

"The best things in life are the ones worth working for! And maybe you think 'I can't do math! Math is hard!'" says Rachel. "Nonsense! All it takes is a little patience, a little confidence and a whole lot of creativity to begin to not only 'get it,' but really *LOVE* math!"

Rachel's four sure-fire ways to help you overcome your fear of a very cool subject are:

Make mistakes. Have you ever noticed how fearless boys can be when they are trying to learn something new? They'll take apart computers, break delicate instruments, laugh and shout until they figure it out! Well, girls can do that, too! Don't be afraid to make mistakes in the name of math and science. Experimentation and solving problems are *exactly* what math and science are all about. And don't take "No" for an answer. If you're having problems solving a difficult equation, don't give up! Ask for help, bat around some ideas, and just have fun! You'll get it.

Act now. Don't wait until tomorrow to embrace something that may scare you! Don't put off what you can do today. Taking that first step and telling yourself, "I can do *math*!" is the first big step in conquering your fear of it. By the time girls get to high school, their confidence in math is way too low. Why? Well, sometimes they just don't get the support they need. It's up to you to begin your future *today!* So just start small. Take an online class. (I recommend Girlstart, at www.girlstart.com, a very cool site for girls with free online classes!) Ask your friends and family for help with homework.

Try something new. So you think math can be kind of boring? Well, tell that to an astronaut, or a deep sea explorer, or a millionaire! Math has *lots* of applications in everyday life *and* it can help you pursue your wildest dreams. Find new passions, and you'll find that math can help you achieve any goal!

Have fun. The best thing that you can do to foster your new love of math is to *have fun!* That's right . . . this isn't your grandpa's math class anymore. From Web sites to starting your own business to finding your true passion in life, math is there to help you all

Test tubes! Experiments! Making potions! Science time . . .

Carletta Ooton is the vice president for quality at Bath & Body Works. She uses science every day in her job, developing and testing what she calls "lotions and potions." Carletta says:

I had a passion for science early, even though my teachers were basically telling me, "No, you shouldn't." My high school teachers really pushed the typical "girl type" classes and kept shoving home ec at me, but I took chemistry and ecology and ended up getting a master's degree in microbiology. It has paid off for me.

Don't be intimidated by science. Science is part of your everyday life. You bake a cake—you've got scientific principles going on. You never know where science is going to pop up. Have you ever noticed that on *Who Wants to Be a Millionaire*, every fourth question is a science one?

Pick a science that interests you. You don't have to love all sciences. Don't think, "I don't like math so science isn't for me, either." There are sciences that deal with people and with animals, so if you're not into chem you might get into a life science, such as biology, physiology, or zoology.

along your merry way! One of the most fun things to do with math is to teach it to others! Sure, *you* can be a teacher for someone who is not quite as skilled as you are. This will not only help someone else learn and thrive, it will remind you that you are *all that!*

◎ Change a Diaper ◎

Sooner or later, it's likely to happen.

It's stinky. It's messy. It might gross you out.

But, especially if you babysit, it's something that's got to get done.

You have to change a diaper.

My twin sister, Jennifer Roy, is an author for teens. She wrote *Romantic Breakup: It's Not the End of the World, Difficult People,* and other books. And she used to be a teacher. But she's working her most important job now: She just became a mom (and made me an aunt—yea!). So she is totally immersed in baby stuff right now. Here is her professional diaper advice.

1. Get ready. Get all the supplies together before you put the baby on the changing table or area:

   • Diaper

   • Wipes or warm, damp washcloth

   • Diaper rash ointment, if needed

   • Pins (if you're using a cloth diaper)

   • A baby toy (to hand to the baby to distract her)

2. Wash and dry your hands.

3. Cover the changing area with a cover or a towel.

4. Lay the baby on his back, and remove the old diaper. Hold on to the baby at all times.

5. Smile, sing, be nice to the baby. It may not be an enjoyable experience for him, but try to make it as pleasant as possible. Smaller babies may like having your hand or a stuffed animal

---

VERY IMPORTANT: Do not leave a child alone on a changing table for even one second. Hold him, even if he isn't squirmy, and even if you get grossed out and overcome by fumes. Take no chances.

on their bellies to make them feel more secure. Older babies may like to hold a toy.

6. Place the diaper out of the child's kick-
    ing and grabbing area (or it will get
    even messier). Hold the baby's legs to-
    gether gently at the ankles with one
    hand. Try to slide and fold the diaper
    off and out so the yuk doesn't fall out
    when you pick the diaper up later. (Yes,
    you will have to pick it up later.)

7. Gently use the wipes to clean the baby.
    Put the wipes with the used diaper. Girls
    should be wiped from front to back. Boys,
    back to front.

> The most important lessons to learn in life are ones that can't be taught in school.
>
> —Maura, 13, Ohio

Tip for Changing Baby Boys: Air can make a baby boy need to go again. Lay the clean diaper on top of the boy so he doesn't spray you!

8. Take the clean diaper and check for the front. Lay the diaper
    under the baby and bring it up through his legs. Pull the top
    over and hold snugly, but not too tight. If it is a disposable
    diaper, pull the sticky tabs open and fasten them on each
    side. If it is a cloth diaper, pin the diaper closed on each side.
    Use your hand to protect the baby from getting stuck with
    the pin.

9. Re-tape the old disposable diaper up into a nice neat little pack-
    age. Cloth diapers could be rinsed out or put in a bag or what-
    ever the mom instructed you to do with it.

10. Take the baby off the changing table and put in a baby-safe
    place.

11. Toss the diaper in the Diaper Genie or into the trash.

12. Wash your hands.

Be a Good Babysitter

- Always be on time.
- Pay attention to the kid(s).
- Bring things like toys and games for the kids to play with.
- If you've had a tough time babysitting two kids, then just babysit one kid until you feel comfortable.
- Don't be mean or spank the kids. If they are out of control, call their parents.
- Tell the parents nice or funny things the kids did.
- Don't watch TV, or do anything that will distract you from the kids.
- Know first aid and CPR.
- Don't answer the door.
- Know numbers to contact the parents, neighbors, or emergency personnel such as the police, fire department, and poison control.
- Keep a phone nearby in case of emergency.
- Don't eat all the food in the house.
- Don't invite your friends or BF over. Follow all the instructions left for you, but make it more fun (like read them extra stories at bedtime and eat healthy snacks—but maybe not *all* the vegetables). Have pajama parties with the kids.
- Wash the dishes and straighten up the house, even if the mess wasn't made when you were there.
- Tell the parents everything that happened, bad and good.
- Tell the parents how cute their kids are.

—Courtesy of Jenny, 14, Ohio;
Ami, 16, Washington; Jackie, 17, Wisconsin

◎ Unclog the Toilet ◎

You are having dinner at your BF's house. You have to, you know, *Go!*
You try to hold it for a while, but nope. You *really* have to go.
You excuse yourself to the bathroom, do your thing. You flush the
toilet. But instead of the water level going down . . . it starts going
up, up, and threatens to overflow.

Potential Humiliation Factor: I'd give this one a 10!

Okay, you thought you were going to skip this one. I mean, who
wants to read about toilets? But I got your attention, and now you
see why you need to know this info. Prepare ahead for this Most
Embarrassing Moment by reading what to do.

Kay Keating from Toiletology.com to the rescue! She gives this
advice: "In most cases the water will stop running before overflowing. Many toilet bowls are designed in such a way that they will
usually hold the entire contents of the tank without overflowing."

First: Don't flush again! Or it probably *will* overflow. You
must wait until the water level drops to normal. If it doesn't drop to
normal, then you need to find out what is blocking the bowl. But
under no circumstances should you flush again.

Unfortunately, this is about where the advice ends as far as being in someone else's house. Because there really isn't a way out of
the embarrassing problem, but at least your, um, toilet water isn't
overflowing. Now you have to let someone know there is a problem.
Hopefully his mom is easy to confide in quietly and won't make a
fuss about it!

If you're in your own home, you can try to fix it yourself for extra GirlWise points.

Quickly turn the water off under the tank. You might have
a shutoff on the wall under the tank. If not, remove the tank lid and
lift up on the float ball or cup. Then have someone else turn the water off at the main shutoff. (This assumes the problem is a clog in
the toilet. If the problem is a backed-up sewer, then turning the water off isn't going to help.)

If you have dropped something in the toilet and accidentally flushed it away, try to retrieve it. Say you dropped a brush in the toilet bowl. You can put your hand inside a large plastic trash bag and try to retrieve the item with your fingertips. It's not always possible, but it's worth a try. Don't force your hand too far into the hole.

Try the plunger or force cap. There are plungers especially made for toilets. One has a cone on the bottom; another has a bellows, which allows for more air to be exerted on the clog. Position the plunger over the large hole in the bowl and push down. Start slowly when using a plunger on a backed-up toilet, then gently build intensity. Develop intensity by gradually pressing more forcefully and pulling back faster. Repeat this as many times as necessary to dislodge the clog. Plunging usually works.

If those don't work . . . time to call the plumber!

✖ Do Laundry ✖

How do you do your laundry? Do you toss it on the floor or in a laundry basket until Mom or Dad comes along and takes care of it?

How nice for you! Will they do mine, too?

But face it: Sooner or later, you're going to have to do your laundry yourself. And you'd better do it right, or you might end up facing "laundry-mergencies," such as:

- White clothes turned colors!
- Overflowing washing machine!
- Shredded shorts!
- Shrunken shirts!

Save yourself from Clothing Catastrophes! Listen to Timi Gleason, an executive coach whose highly organized daughter wanted to know how to do her own laundry rather than wait for her mom to get around to doing it.

Step 1: Divide your clothes into piles.

1. **Darks.** Colored clothes bleed dye. If you mix them with white clothes, you may get pink underwear. Darks should be washed in cold water and dried on low temperature, or they will shrink and bleed heavily.

   Red, dark blue, and purple items are at high risk for bleeding into whites.

2. **Whites.** These are fabrics that are completely white, usually cotton, and highly absorbent.

3. **Delicates.** Delicates can't be washed in a normal cycle. They either need to be hand-washed or put into a delicate cycle in the washing machine. If washed with regular clothes, the fabric may tear, get a run in it, lose its shape, or shrink. Check the labels. Frequently, delicates must be dried by air and laid flat. Hosiery and certain sweaters should be laid out to air dry. Some delicates can be dried in the "air only" cycle (no heat) if they can keep their shape.

   Some delicates should only be hand-washed. Hand-wash items are just too delicate to be mixed with heavier items without being ruined. If you aren't sure, be on the safe side. Some hosiery, sweaters, and underwear are too delicate to be put into a machine. Hosiery can sometimes be put into mesh bags and protected from tearing in a washing machine, but that takes experimentation.

4. **Dry Cleaning.** When you are buying your clothes, before you put your money down, look at the cleaning requirements. If the label says "Dry Clean," then that's an added expense to think about. These clothes may shrink or lose their shape or bleed

---

Hint: **If you notice any rashes on your legs or on your neck, consider that your detergent may be causing an allergic reaction on your skin, and that you may be putting too much in (and it's not getting washed out completely).**

Hint: Are your socks disappearing? They could be going out with the washer rinse cycle. If you notice problems, put socks in a mesh bag so they can't escape so easily!

---

their color if washed in water. You can buy kits in the supermarket for effectively dry cleaning sweaters and some shirts in your dryer. Jackets and some types of clothing are best taken to a commercial dry cleaner, where they will be pressed and made to look like new again.

Step 2: Load the washing machine.

Start the water running first, and then put in the detergent. Put in the amount of detergent recommended on the label. Add too much, and your washing machine might overflow with suds. Notice that you can control the level of the water in the washer, so small loads need less soap. Use your common sense and read the label on the detergent box.

If you don't add the detergent before you put in the clothes, you might get stuck with permanent bleach or detergent spots on your clothes. Also, some water has harsh chemicals in it that can be neutralized by putting the detergent in first. Try to remember to do this. If you forget, be sure you don't pour the detergent directly onto the clothes in the water. Let the water swish around after adding the soap and before adding the clothes.

Be very careful about using bleach. Get some help with what proper amounts are and when you shouldn't add bleach. Never add regular bleach to colored clothes.

Step 3: Dry.

Put your wet clothes in the dryer. Remember to pull out any clothes that need to be laid flat to dry. Toss in any fabric softener sheets you might use.

Keep the lint trap on your dryer emptied. If you don't, the dryer will take forever to dry the clothes.

Wash towels together and don't mix them with sweaters. The sweaters will pick up the lint.

Set up a spot to hang freshly dried shirts and pants so they don't get wrinkled. Remove clothes from the dryer promptly so they can be smoothed out by hand and don't need ironing.

Don't ever leave wet clothes sitting in a washer or dryer for more than a day. They will mildew (get all moldy) from sitting wet, and you'll have to rewash them to remove the bacteria. Try to remove clothes from the dryer promptly (while they are still warm), and get them laid out or hung up so they look good. Hang up shirts on a hanger, smooth the collar out, button the top button, and straighten out the shoulders so that, as the shirt cools, it "dries" as you want it to look.

Shake out towels and sheets to remove static cling and to uncover lost socks and underwear that may be clinging to other items.

Empty mesh bags after washing and lay the delicates on the dryer to air dry. Or put your mesh bag into the dryer if the items are hardy enough.

Most modern fabrics don't do well on very hot drying temperatures. Towels may be the only exception. Almost everything else does better on low, which is pretty warm, too.

You also might get a laundry rack to air-dry delicates. You can set it up in a corner of your bathroom or in your tub and fold it up when you don't need it. They are easy to fold up and store in closets. You can use them to hang out freshly dried shirts and pants, too. You can find racks in the hanger or laundry section of stores like Target, Wal-Mart, or a home decoration store.

Chapter **4**

Be in Control

✧ Shake Hands ✧

You're interviewing for a job.

You're meeting your BFF's father.

You want to look in control the first time you meet someone.

One of the first things you can do to make a strong impression is to shake someone's hand. Yes, girls should shake hands, too. They say you can tell a lot about a person by his or her handshake. I know I cringe when I shake someone's hand and it's all limp and wimpy. Or even creepier, when someone keeps holding on to your hand well after the handshake should be over. Yuk.

You can do the handshake thing right. Use the Power Hand Shake, courtesy of Sherry Maysonave, president of Empowerment Enterprises and author of *Casual Power.*

Step 1: Extend your hand for a handshake. Don't hesitate to hold your hand out first.

Step 2: Grasp. Slide your palm all the way into the other person's hand to the end of their palm.

Step 3: Give their hand a firm grip. This doesn't mean that you try to break their fingers, but it does mean that you give their hand a firm grip. Lifeless, limp, dead-fish handshakes silently scream that you are insecure, possibly immature. It certainly does nothing to project confidence.

Step 4: Shake. Shake firmly. Don't give a wet, limp fish handshake. Look people in the eyes when shaking their hands. The power handshake should not last more than two or three seconds. Don't shake more than three times. If the other person doesn't let go of your hand within four or five seconds, this signals she or he is either insecure or has another reason for hanging on to you. Be cautious! This person may not know how to shake, or might be untrustworthy. Don't say anything, but file this incident away in your mind.

✤ Give a Speech ✤

Lots of reports say that the number one fear people have is this: giving a speech!

Standing up in front of all those people. Everyone looking at you. Waiting for you to make a fool of yourself. Just waiting to laugh at you.

It is really hard to stand up in front of a bunch of people and talk. What if you bore them to death? What if they laugh at you? What if you make a total and complete idiot of yourself?

You won't if you take the following advice. (I *promise!*)

Merrie Spaeth knows speeches: She's written them, even worked at the White House helping former President Reagan with them. (And he was *way* well-known for his speeches.) Now she owns a business teaching people how to give speeches. If she can help the president, she can help you. Here's Merrie's advice for *your* big moment:

> **Don't regret not doing something when you had the chance. Make this your goal.**
> —Whitney, 17, Ohio

What an honor! You've been selected to make a speech for Presidents' Day (or whatever) in front of your school. But, if this is such a privilege, how come you feel the flu coming on?

Run to the bathroom. Look in the mirror, and say, "I *can* do this." Now say it again—louder (might as well start learning to project)—"I *can* do this!" Good. Because you can.

Think three—three elements of planning a successful speech:

Know what you're going to say.

Let's start with what you're going to say. Imagine that you see your best bud Kate after your speech at assembly. You can't believe it, she missed your speech? Kate claims she's devastated and is dying to know what you said in the one minute before the bell rings to get to your next class. What would you tell Kate you said?

You need three or four headlines. What are the three or four top messages you want people to remember?

These are your beginning *and* your end points. Then, you bring up each one as you speak and go into it in more detail.

Practice how you're going to say it.

Once you've gotten your speech down in written form, you can type it up in *big* letters (24-point bolded type) and use it as a script to glance down at. Don't split paragraphs between pages, and don't staple the pages.

Or, you can reduce the speech to an outline or key words. Do what makes you comfortable (except ask someone else to give your speech!). And don't feel you have to memorize it.

Put a reminder to smile—Happy Face!—on each page. Each time you see it, your face will lighten up. It's like having your own personal coach.

Rehearse.

Now, here's how to guarantee success. Stand up and practice. Bribe your friends with munchies and invite them over to listen. Then do The Speech in front of a few people you *don't* know. (Think you'll die of embarrassment? You won't. But you will "die" on the stage if you get up there and haven't rehearsed.)

Here are some more tips from Merrie for giving your speech:

- Look at the audience (not your notes).

- Project your voice so you can be heard.

Hint: **If you look up at the beginning, when you make a major point, and at the end of a sentence, you create the impression that you've been looking up all along.**

- Look as if you're enjoying yourself. Relax! This is a learned art. You can be knotted inside, but keep smiling and only you will know.

If you find your hands take on a life of their own and gravitate to the podium, step back. (This is why you have to be able to see what you've written from farther away.)

When you do look out, don't scan the audience. This only makes them wonder what you've spotted. Talk to one person at a time, and really pour your heart out to them. Every time you look up or down, pick another person. (Obviously, pick people all over the auditorium, not just your pals in the small group halfway back on the left side.)

Does this ever get easy? After a while, it may. But you learn to make it look easy.

Think of it this way: You can speak to one person, right? An audience is just made up of a bunch of "one persons."

❂ Speak with a Powerful Voice ❂

Do you know someone who talks in a high-pitched cutesy voice that makes her sound like a weak little girl? Or do you know someone who talks in a whisper so you can hardly hear her? Your voice plays a part in the impression you make. Your voice can help you sound confident, capable, cool, and in control—or the opposite.

Not convinced? Okay, then think about your different teachers. Aren't there some with great speaking voices? They make you actually want to pay attention. Then there's the teacher who goes on and on in the same tone of voice . . . BO-ring. And the teacher who talks so quietly that it's hard to hear. So you tune him or her out.

It's not just teachers. Your voice is sending a message to your friends and anyone you talk to. Make your words powerful. Speaking coach Elanna Donovan can help you do it. Here are her suggestions:

Find your natural voice. It is often lower than the voice you usually use, which can be constricted by tension, habit, and shallow breathing. Here's an exercise to help you find the natural pitch of your voice. Bend over and say, "Hello." Now, work to maintain that pitch as you stand up straight and inhale deeply. It takes practice. This is the voice you should try to use when you are speaking. A lower, modulated voice is generally easier on the ear. Easier on the ear means your audience will listen to you longer before they tune out.

Strengthen your voice. An excellent exercise to strengthen your voice is to sing. Sing high, sing low, sing the musical scale. It increases your speaking vocal range and helps with your breath control.

Take a deep breath and let it out slowly while you say a long sentence of your choice. Do this until you can maintain the same speaking volume from beginning to end of sentence (without rushing the words at the end). Increase the length of the sentence. When you do this, place your hand on your diaphragm. You can feel your body filling up with air. As you speak, you can feel the air going out. You'll be speaking from the diaphragm, and this will help your powerful voice.

Eliminate the "whiskers." Hi, um, do you want to, ah, be my lab partner, ya know? Get rid of all those *ums, ahs,* and *you knows.* Toastmasters calls those words "whiskers." So many people use these without thinking. Whiskers can distract from your message. They also can drive a listener crazy.

Don't make everything sound like a question. Girls' voices often rise at the end, as if they are asking a question. When you do this, you sound unsure of yourself: "I finished the report?" "I want a sandwich?" Lose that questioning tone! People won't take you seriously if you sound as though you are questioning your own statements.

> If you try to impress someone else, do something a certain way to be like everything else, or stop being true to yourself, you will lose yourself. And it's hard to figure out who you are when you're already gone.
>
> —Harmony, 17, Pennsylvania

"Sorry . . . sorry . . . sorry . . ."

Don't destroy your credibility right at the start by starting off with an apology. "This is probably a stupid idea, but . . ." "This might bore you, but . . ." "This is a dumb question, but . . ." "I don't know why I'm saying this, but . . ." Just say it! No apologies!

Vary your speaking style. Have you ever listened to someone who talks in a monotone? That is, she just drones on and on without raising or lowering her voice. Make sure you don't bore your audience like that. Speaking with a powerful voice is like music. An interesting piece of music uses many different notes on the scale. The pacing and volume of the words vary. Listen to a good singer or speaker. It's not a monotonous delivery. It keeps your attention. The more confident and impassioned the singer or speaker, the more powerful she is.

If you think your speaking style is too boring, get a tape recorder. Read some poetry or a magazine paragraph into a tape recorder. Next, close your eyes and describe a favorite relative or friend into the tape recorder. See and describe that person. Now listen to the difference in your voice. What do you notice? When you are describing someone you know, how do you sound? More animated, more alive, more passionate, more focused? It doesn't matter what you are feeling, but you'll notice that your feelings are reflected in your voice. This is great. It is *not* boring.

◎ Find a Mentor ◎

Who's a great person to help you plan your future? No, not a fortune teller. A mentor. Suppose you could pick the brain of someone who has your dream job, goes to the college you want to go to, or simply seems happy with herself. Think of all the mistakes you could avoid, the inside scoop you could get. Well, why can't you find a mentor?

Here's some advice from our mentor on mentors, Dawn Nocera of EducatingJane.com:

> A mentor is someone who helps you achieve your goals. A mentor might be your neighbor, a teacher, an aunt, an older sister . . . someone you admire. Your mentor should listen to you, care about you, and be someone you trust. Think, "Hm, I want to be more like this person. . . ." Fess up, you know that sometimes you think, "Nyah, I can't ever . . . (fill in the blank: "go to that college," "get a job as a such and such," "be successful"). You can look for someone who's been there, done that. And she can help show you how!

Here are some kinds of mentors:

Career Mentor: *Helps you plan ahead for a career you have your eye on.*

College Mentor: *Helps you plan to go to college and succeed.*

Job Mentor: *Helps you get ahead in a job you have.*

Life Mentor: *Helps you get what you want out of life.*

BMF? Best Mentors Forever? Not necessarily. You can have a short-term mentor to help get you through some quick stuff, too. Have a debate competition? Ask a local politician for pointers. Trying out for cheerleading? Find a college student who used to be on the squad. Want to improve your pitch? Ask a coach to give you some one-on-one.

"Being exposed to a successful, positive adult is a great way to help you become one," says Dawn.

Here are ways you can get yourself a mentor:

Find a mentor. There are a couple of ways to go about getting a mentor. Sometimes, they just sort of come along. Like, you are in a play and your drama teacher starts helping you out and sharing her experiences when she was an actress. But you don't have to just wait to stumble into a mentor.

Go looking. Start your search by making a list of things you want in a mentor. Do you want someone who can help you deal with a difficult family situation? Do you want someone to help you learn about a job? Do you want an athletic mentor to help you stay fit? Do you want a mentor to help you along your spiritual path?

Make a list. Next make a list of all the people you know who might have something to offer. You could start your own address book with everyone's name, address, and phone number on each card, along with a description of how they might be able to help. Brainstorm here: You might include parents, relatives, neighbors, teachers, coaches, counselors, ministers and rabbis, community leaders, and local businesswomen on your list. You don't have to stay local; you can get a mentor online and exchange e-mails with her or him. List everyone that you respect, admire, or think is cool, smart, and a worthy role model.

You don't have limit your list to women and older girls; you could have a couple of males on your list to cover topics like brother–sister stuff and male points of view. (Check with your parents before you approach anyone they don't know! Seriously, you are putting your trust into a mentor so you have to make sure the person is trustworthy.) Include on the list anyone who may be able to help you find a mentor, too.

Ask. You have two ways to go about this. You can ask the person directly, "Would you like to be my mentor?" If you do this, be prepared to explain why you chose her (or him) and what you expect from the person. For example, tell her whether you want to talk on the phone every two weeks for a half hour about your classes, or if you want to follow her around at her job for a day.

Or, you can use the indirect approach. Call or e-mail with one question. "I really want to go to your college next year. Do you have any advice on how I can get in?" Once you break the ice, you two might click, and then you can ease into a mentor relationship.

I'm mentoring a senior at my local high school, Whitney. She's a writer who wants to get published. So, great! I suggested she write some pieces of advice for this book, and she did it right away. Ta-da! She's about to be published!

Rejection!

Not everyone has time or is up to being a mentor. So be prepared for someone to say, "Nope, sorry." Be gracious and thank the person anyway. Ask if she or he knows someone who might help you out. If the person still is unresponsive, move on.

For example, you might e-mail a popular author and tell him you want to get published. You check and check your in-box, and wait and wait. The same thing usually happens when you contact movie stars and other celebs. Don't take it personally.

◎ Be in Charge ◎ of Your Financial Life

Have you fallen for the whole Cinderella theme? You know, someday your prince will come, whisk you away to his castle, take care of you so you have no worries, and you two will live happily ever after? A lot of girls and women buy into this dream. But a dream is all this fantasy should be, because this is one dream that can turn into a nightmare. You might be starting off not thinking much about money, except what it can buy you. You spend the money, and you don't worry about it.

Serious, serious mistake. You need to know how to take care of your money because that's a major way you get to take care of *you*.

Barbara Stanny is author of *Prince Charming Isn't Coming* and *Secrets of Six-Figure Women*. She's also the daughter of the "R" in H&R Block. If you're not a money person, that won't mean much to you, but picture 19 million people, and that's how many people H&R Block helps with their taxes and money management. It's a huge, HUGE company. Her father is one of the biggest names in the financial field, but he told Barbara not to think about money. He'd take care of her, then later she'd get married and her husband would take over.

So Barbara not only had a huge trust fund, but she married a guy who was a lawyer in the financial field. She thought he was her Prince Charming. Sounds like she was set for life, right? She thought so. But nope, the guy gambled all her money away. She lost a fortune, even owing a million dollars that she had to pay back.

This made her realize that *she* had to learn to be smart about money—even though she felt dumb about financial things. So she thinks every girl—and moms, too—needs to know some basics about finance so every female can be financially secure. Barbara has some great info on how you can "un-dumb" yourself about money:

> If you have the means, donate money, food, or toys.
> —Trinity, 18, Florida

Recognize the power of money. Money talks. We may not like it, but money runs the world. Money elects our politicians; it determines what we own and where we live.

Being smart about money is not only about being rich (although that is a fine goal); it's about having security. Money gives you the freedom to make choices—such as leaving a job you hate because you have money saved for a backup plan. You can choose to travel, try new things.

Know the five things you have to do to be financially independent. Here they are:

1. Earn more.
2. Spend less.
3. Save sufficiently.
4. Invest wisely.
5. Give generously.

Talk about money. Girls are taught that money is this taboo topic. Boys aren't born knowing about finances, but they're expected to know it so they learn it. Girls often don't. Get over your fear of money. Start a group for girls and your moms and invest or talk about money.

Don't feel stupid starting at the beginning. The teacher who says, "There are no dumb questions" is right. Even the most basic question is okay: "Um, what does the word 'finances' mean?" (Webster's says finances are "money or other liquid resources of a government, business, group, or individual.") Understanding finance can take a lot of time.

Read about finance. Read the newspaper. There are great books for people of all ages. Look for books by authors such as Jayne Pearl, Joline Godfrey, and Neale S. Godfrey.

Find someone to teach you. It might be a family member or your economics teacher. Or, you might sign up for a free class on finance. Or, ask your mom to take you to a financial advisor. Ask away . . . and find out what you need to know.

Buy stock. Choose a stock for a company where you shop or whose products you like. My daughter owns Gap stock, and when she shops there, she knows she owns a part of it. My other daughter drives a Ford, and owns Ford stock as well as stock in AT&T. You can buy stock online. For example, you can visit the McDonald's Web site, go to the investor relations section, and buy a share of stock.

Ask for money gifts. Ask for stock in a favorite store. One share of stock in a favorite company, such as Nike or Sony, doesn't cost much and is a fun gift.

Save. You don't get rich from what you make. You get rich from what you save. Have a percentage taken right out of your paycheck or allowance so you don't even miss it. I told my daughters, "I want

Beware! Nothing erodes a sense of self-esteem more than a lack of money. You're always worrying about paying your bills, about credit card statements coming, about not being able to buy something you need.

Hint: "Spend intelligently. A lot of times you'll be at the mall with your friends and you'll all go, "Oh, that's *so* cute!" So everyone buys it. But wait: First ask yourself if you really need it or if you can live without it."

—Anna, 17, and friends Arianne, Henrike, and Heissam

you to save a little of what you make automatically in a savings account." One saved up enough money to travel for six months.

Limit credit card use. Credit cards give a false sense of security. You can get into huge debt and not be able to dig yourself out. But the interest rates make it so you wind up paying way more than you would if you paid right away.

Think of money as a way to help others. Have big dreams of what you want to do with your life. And then see what role money can play in helping you achieve your goals. A checkbook can accomplish many things. You can help charities and people in need. If you're passionate about a cause, think of the satisfaction you'll feel writing a check to help.

It's so powerful when you see the numbers growing in your savings and investments, and you can say, "This is mine!" There's no greater feeling of independence than having a stash of money.

✵ Run for School Office ✵

"Vote Julia—She's Cool-ia!"

Hey, I was in fourth grade when I put that campaign slogan all over posters in my classroom and gave a speech on why I thought our class should get two hamsters (not just one!).

And I won the election! Yes, even with that slogan.

Just call me "Madam President" (of Mrs. Brefka's fourth-grade class).

Student council. Class president. Class representative. Have you considered running for school office?

Play the Stock Market

First, read the section earlier in this chapter on Being in Charge of Your Financial Life. That will give you the lead-in for this section. Okay, done with that? Ready, set, go!

When you buy a stock, you buy shares in a company. This means that you own part of the business. You are an investor because you have invested in the company. The stock market is where stocks are bought and sold.

You can buy or sell stocks at any time. You can buy stocks through companies called stock brokerages, like Merrill Lynch or Charles Schwab. You can also buy directly from the company in direct purchase programs. Or, you can buy a mutual fund, which is a big collection of stocks and bonds. Mutual funds can be safer than buying individual shares of a company, because a mutual fund has experts who pick the stocks for you. A mutual fund helps you diversify your investment. Diversification means investing in different kinds of investments to lessen risk and spread out in a variety of investments that react differently.

Stock prices move up and down, based on how investors feel about the world. When the economy is doing well, it is a boom. When the stock market is up for a long time, it's

"Go for it," says Congresswoman Deborah Pryce. Congresswoman Pryce represents the 15th District of Ohio and currently is the highest-ranking Republican woman in the House of Representatives. She was on student council when she was a teen.

"Holding office is a great way to experience what true responsibility is," says Congresswoman Pryce. "You have the ability to change things for the better. You have the opportunity to help others. When you are a leader, there's so much you can do to make a difference."

called a "bull market." When it is doing poorly, it is a recession. When the stock market is down for a long time, it's called a "bear market." A market that goes up and down a lot is called "volatile."

When you buy stock, you buy for what the company will be in the future. If the company does better in the future than it did in the past, the price of the shares goes up, which increases your investment and makes you money. People on Wall Street (where the stock markets are) try to predict what a company will earn. If companies are doing well and they are growing faster than most other companies, stock prices go up.

Stocks tend to give you a better return (more money back) than a savings account. But there is more risk involved in the purchase of stocks. The stock you buy can go down in value as well as up. A savings account doesn't lose value, but it also won't give you as much potential to make more money, either. If you're interested in investing, you can find tons of info online. Many investment firms offer free seminars, and some have free books.

—Mary Lisanti is the chief investment officer
of Domestic Equities ING Funds
and a portfolio manager of growth mutual funds.

Once you decide to run for election, there are ways you can make your campaign the best it can be. Congresswoman Pryce shares how to run a successful campaign:

Get to know your constituents. In politics, the people who can vote for you are called your constituents. In your case, they'll be your classmates. If you attend a smaller school, you might know everyone. In a larger school, you should make the effort to get to know people you don't ordinarily know. It's hard to get elected with just a small group of friends.

Identify who has influence in different groups at school. Once you identify leaders of different groups and cliques, you can focus on getting to know them. Often once you get the leaders on your side, their flock will follow.

People respond to personal contact. In my race for my first leadership position in Congress, I made it a point to have a conversation with every single person involved. Whether they agreed with my viewpoint or not, it gave them the chance to get to know me as a person. The value in this is that whether you win or lose, you've gotten to know new people and even made some new friends.

> Attend school functions. You'll look back on the memories and smile.
>
> —Jessica, 18, California

Build a cabinet. It's hard to run a campaign alone. You need to have a group to help you. In politics, it's called your kitchen cabinet, or cabinet for short. Find people who believe in you. Your group shouldn't just be your best friends and people in your usual group. Reach out to different segments of your school society and make your cabinet as diverse as you can. They will help you with the segments of the school population you wouldn't normally hang out with—you want to be a representative of all groups.

Make a game plan. Hold a meeting of your cabinet. Figure out how each person can help your campaign. Brainstorm how to best use each person's talents and interests. Are they artistic? Can they help write speeches? Raise money? Make a Web site? Put the plan on paper so everyone knows what is expected of him or her.

Get the answers to these questions: What's the time frame for the election? How much budget do you have for the campaign? Do you need to raise money for the campaign? How many votes do you need to get elected?

Develop your platform. Your platform is the statement of what you are planning to do if you are elected. You need to let everyone know your plans. You also want your classmates to know your qualifications and why you think you are the best candidate for the job.

Pick three or four important points that you want people to know about you. Make them easy to remember. Focus on points that will affect the quality of your classmates' lives. You want them to think that their lives will be better if they elect you. Show that you have vision, that you will interact with them after the campaign is over. Show you're not just about campaign promises; you are a true leader. Show that you are focused and dedicated.

Challenge your classmates. Stand for a cause: Show them you have a vision to do things they can't do alone. Whether it's volunteering, planning a class trip to Europe, starting a new club, raising funds for charity . . . involve them!

Get your message out. Determine how you can best get visibility. If you're in a big school, it will be difficult to reach everybody individually. Send your team out to get your message across. Have them try to get your classmates to commit to voting for you. Once someone says yes, don't neglect them. Check back later and ask for their vote again, in case another candidate has gotten to them in the meantime.

If possible, send a note or e-mail to the classmates who agreed to vote for you. It might say, "Thanks for agreeing to support my candidacy. I promise to do a good job and be a positive leader for you."

Depending on your budget and time frame, you might also get visibility with:

- Signs to post at school and other places students hang out
- Buttons your supporters can wear
- Brochures to pass out to your classmates
- Postcards you send with a personal note to the recipient
- Web sites
- E-mails with a personal message included

When I ran for one of my early offices, I made up postcards that my supporters could send out to other people. They said something like: "I'm Suzie, I'm supporting Deborah Pryce. I hope you will support her, too." It's always effective to have other people ask for your vote, rather than just you.

Congratulations!
You won! Be gracious. Start right to work and don't lose momentum. Ask advice and get help if you need it. Remember, it's a new role and nobody expects you to know it all. Keep your promises. Always work with integrity.

Bummer.
You lost. Be gracious. Congratulate your opponent. Evaluate what worked and didn't work. What can you learn from it? Follow up with your new friends, especially your supporters. Keep your plans and lists; they'll come in handy next time!

Stay positive. You will want to stay positive throughout your campaign. But know that negative campaigning is a way of life in politics these days. You might even face negativity in a school campaign, such as put-downs and dirty tricks from your opponents. The best way to respond is with grace and aplomb. Don't allow someone to provoke you to participate in behavior you will later regret. Don't get down into the "mud" with them; rise above it. And whether you win or lose, be gracious.

◇ Get a ◇ College Scholarship

College is seriously expensive. And you have to pay for it somehow.

My advice is to try author Kelly Tanabe's way of paying for college: scholarships—free money that you don't have to pay back. Kelly won enough scholarships to leave Harvard debt-free. Debt-free?!? Trust me, she knew what she was doing. I left college and graduate school buried under major debt. I truly thought you had to be the class valedictorian to get a scholarship so I didn't bother trying. Since I'm no role model for this one, I will get out of the way and let Kelly tell you what to do:

With college costing as much as $30,000 per year, it is no surprise that you and your parents might be feeling the pressure.

So does that mean you should sacrifice your dream college and just go to the cheapest school? Absolutely not! There is another way that an enterprising girl can pay for college, and it doesn't involve asking, "Do you want fries with that order?"

The answer is scholarships, and there are millions of dollars out there waiting to be won. But it takes work to get your share of this scholarship pie. Here are four steps to winning scholarships and earning the lifelong gratitude of your parents.

Step 1: Lose the "I don't have good grades" excuse for not applying.

One of the biggest myths about scholarships is that they only go to the valedictorians.

The truth is the vast majority of awards are based on much more than your grades. While most awards have a minimum GPA requirement, it is often low enough for most students to qualify. When it comes to choosing a winner, scholarship judges won't care that you got a C in Physics. What matters is that you show why you deserve to win.

And being younger than a senior is also not a valid excuse. There are plenty of awards for underclasswomen, such as these:

Imation Computer Arts Scholarship (www.imation.com)

National History Day Contest (www.thehistorynet.com)

National High School Oratorical Contest (www.legion.org)

Discover Card Tribute Award Scholarship (www.aasa.org/discover.htm)

> Don't screw up your junior year. I'm a senior now and struggling with getting into the colleges I want to go to because I blew things off.
>
> —Patricia, 17, Massachusetts

Ayn Rand Essay Contests (www.aynrand.org)

Optimist International Essay Contest (www.optimist.org)

Now is the best time to get in on the action.

Step 2: Find scholarships in your own backyard.

So you've decided that you want to win some free cash for college. Next, you need to do some detective work to find awards. When looking for scholarships, most students immediately turn to the Internet or directories of national awards. However, some of the best scholarships are in your backyard: your community.

Before you do anything else, make an appointment with your college guidance counselor. This person knows all about local scholarships given to students at your school. Next, think about all of the clubs and activities that you are in and find out whether they offer awards to members. Don't just limit yourself to what's on campus. Look at local businesses, service organizations, politicians, and churches. Often these groups give awards to students in the community. Open the phone book and call some. Finally, have your parents ask their employers, unions, and organizations to which they belong about scholarships.

Once you have exhausted your community, take a look at the scholarship directories found in bookstores and libraries, as well as the free databases on the Internet. Use as many resources as you can to search for scholarships since you never know where you might find one that fits you.

Scholarships have been found on credit card bills, on television, and even on candy bar wrappers!

Step 3: Show the judges why you deserve to win.

Imagine that you're a successful businesswoman who belongs to an organization that supports women in business. One way your group achieves this goal is by offering a scholarship. You sit on the judging committee and must sift through a mountain of applications. How do you decide who gets your money? Easy. You look for the applicant who demonstrates an interest in business and women's issues and who has the most promise for the future. In other words you want someone who is just like you—only twenty years younger!

Back to reality. Once you understand this, you know what you need to do to win. If you were applying for this award, you would highlight in your application your desire to major in business, your work experience, or your dedication to women's issues. On the other hand, if you were applying for an award based on service, you would highlight your community service or volunteer work.

The key to winning is to learn who the scholarship organization wants to give its money to (*Big Hint:* The organization usually spells it out in plain English on the application!), and then make sure that every piece of your application—application form, essay, interview, letters of recommendation—shows them why *you* deserve to win.

Step 4: Don't leave money on the table when you apply to college.

Nearly every college gives money to incoming students. The good news is that you often don't need to do anything special to apply. You will automatically be considered for scholarships with your college admission application. Many colleges offer full-tuition scholarships based on your college application. Check out the Web sites of the colleges that you are interested in to see what scholarships are available. Or contact the financial aid office directly to ask. The key is to focus on your admission application.

Beware! In your zeal to find awards, avoid paying for services that charge to find awards. Often they give you nothing better than what you can find for free. To get you started, here are some of the best free scholarship databases on the Internet:

- www.supercollege.com
- www.wiredscholar.com
- www.collegeboard.com

A well-crafted application can make the difference between getting accepted—and getting accepted with a scholarship.

Lastly, it is true that many more students apply for awards than win. It takes time to put together a powerful application. But if you do spend the time on finding awards and applying for them, you *can* win.

Still don't think it's possible? For one of the books that I wrote, I spoke with students who were fanatical about applying for scholarships. Sure, it meant less time to spend with friends, but they won tens of thousands of dollars to pay for college. One student won more than $1 million in scholarships! You have to remember that somebody is going to win these awards, and it might as well be you.

✦ Get Into the College ✦ of Your Choice

So you've researched different colleges. Maybe you visited some campuses. Bought some of the logo sweatshirts. Checked out the college guys.

And now . . . you have a winner! You have chosen a college you want to attend! With a couple of backup choices!

One minor detail—how do you get them to let you in?!

College is where you might be spending, oh, about four years of your life—which is a major commitment. Might as well try to be accepted at one of the places you really want to go. Kelly Tanabe—you read about her in the last section—has a book called *Get Into Any College: Secrets of Harvard Students*. She unveils some of the mystery that surrounds the college admission process for you. Here's her advice:

> What are colleges looking for when they read my application? Who are these admission officers who will decide my fate? Am I placing my future into the hands of some shadowy admission committee that takes perverse pleasure in stamping "Rejected!" on my application?
>
> The truth, fortunately, is much more mundane. Colleges actually *want* to let you in. In fact, college admission officers, those men and women who will evaluate your applica-

tion, essay, grades, test scores, and teacher recommendations truly enjoy working with young people. When admission officers pick up your application, they are looking for reasons to let you into their school. So let's take the mystery out of getting into college and look at what most college admission officers are looking for when deciding whether or not to accept you.

> Soon popularity won't matter. In college, the campus is too big for anyone to care about popularity status.
>
> —Amy, 16, Ohio

Find the right match.

In some ways, colleges are like people. They have their own reputations, personalities, and values. Compare UC Berkeley to the University of Virginia, and you will immediately see and feel a difference in the character and composition of the student body. When college admission officers are looking at your application, one question they have in mind is this: "Will she fit in and be happy at our school?" This means that you need to do your research before you apply to and pick colleges that you feel fit you best. Consider their academic strengths, teaching methods, and campus life rather than just their high ranking in a news magazine. Try to visit the campus so you can sample the environment. Picking the schools that you truly want to attend is the first step to scoring points with the admission officer.

Get to know the college people.

Take every opportunity to shmooze. To share information about their schools, admission officers frequently visit high schools and communities. Think of this as not only your opportunity to learn about the schools, but more importantly to score some brownie points. When you attend, instead of hanging in the back of the room, make your presence known. If you're brave enough, ask questions during the meeting. Or, if not, speak with the admission officer afterward. Make sure that the answers to your questions are not obvious. For example, the admission officers will definitely not be impressed if you ask, "Where is your college located?" Your point in asking questions is to not only learn about the college, but also to share something about yourself. The real secret is that the admission officer you speak with may be the same person to eventually review your application. A brief personal meeting at one of these informational sessions can give you an extra boost.

This also works when you visit colleges. Make arrangements ahead of time to meet with professors or advisors in the department you want to enter. Ask informed questions about the department, classes, and research that the professors are doing. Share how you can see yourself contributing to the field. Not only will you get more information about the major, but the results of your meeting may travel to the admission office.

Focus on your academics.

Academics are King. Your parents may not be right about whom you should date or what time your curfew should be, but they are right about one thing: You need to hit the books. When evaluating your application, an important question that college admission officers ask is this: Can you handle the academic coursework? You can be the most brilliant musician, talented artist, or philanthropic volunteer; but if you can't handle college-level academics, you won't be admitted.

Write a strong essay.

If academics are King, the essay is Queen. While academics are important, the truth is that a lot of applicants meet the college's academic requirements. In fact, many applicants will have similar grades and test scores. So how does an admission officer choose between two students with 3.5 GPAs? Often, the answer is the essay. For each application, you will write anywhere from one to three essays about topics such as your favorite book, a class or other academic experience, an influential person, or the topic of your choice.

This is your opportunity to share something about yourself with the admission officers. It is also the opportunity for you to make your application stand out from the rest. Remember that as you write your essay, you want to share with colleges who you are beyond the facts in your application. The essay is not the time to write a résumé or make a list of all of your extracurricular activities. The essay is your chance to impart what motivates you, what has made you who you are, and why you are different from every other applicant. The key is to write about something that is important to you. When it comes down to it, when you have applicants of equal academic standing, the essay can determine who gets it.

Prepare for the tests.

To apply to college, you will need to take no less than six hours of standardized tests. In general, these include the SAT I or ACT and three SAT II exams. One thing that college admission officers don't like to see is SAT Tunnel Vision, or a preoccupation with test scores. Some students get so focused on test scores that they lose sight of everything else. This is not to say that test scores aren't important; they are. And the best way that you can prepare for them is to use old exams for practice. These are available at www.act.org and www.collegeboard.com. But don't become obsessed with standardized tests.

Follow your passions.

Because colleges want a class of students that is involved in athletics, the arts, and other activities on campus, they consider what you do outside of the classroom to be extremely important. Some students think that there's a secret formula for activities that they should participate in that will be impressive to colleges. The real secret is that you should do what you enjoy. You should dedicate yourself to and excel in the activities that you like. Don't participate in athletics if you hate balls and bats. Don't volunteer at a homeless shelter if you really don't care. Find something that you do care about, and dedicate yourself to it. Admission officers can detect when you do something just to impress them. They really want to see that you do what you are passionate about.

Make your application error-free.

Perfection counts. There are several pieces to college applications, including the forms where you list personal and academic information, teacher recommendations, essays, and transcripts. Your goal when completing your applications is to make them as perfect as possible. This means doing them well before the night before they are due and having someone else review them to check for spelling, grammar, or other mistakes. Putting time into your applications shows colleges that you are serious about being admitted.

Whew! If it seems like a ton of work, it is. But hey, you will be the one spending four or so years at this place. And when you are all settled in on the campus of your choice, it will all have been worthwhile!

✤ Choose a Career ✤

What do you want to be when you grow up?

You've heard that since you were, what, a fetus?

I always thought it was kind of fun to think about what career I would have. My second-grade diary says I was going to be a "gymnastics girl." Interesting career choice for a girl who had never taken a lesson and was well-known for being uncoordinated. Then, my seventh-grade diary says I'm going to be an author. So does my junior-year journal. And hey, it happened. So yup, what you're thinking about now might really happen. You absolutely, definitely do *not* have to feel pressured to choose a career now. (I did about ten other jobs along the way to get here.) But it doesn't hurt to start thinking about it.

Linda Smith is a college professor who counsels people on their career choices. Here are her 5 Wrong Ways to Choose a Career—and 5 Right Ones.

1. Wrong Way: Listen to everyone else.

Right Way: Get to know yourself. "Know thyself." This advice from fifth-century B.C. Greek philosopher Socrates is still good 2,500 years later—and is perhaps the best advice you will find anywhere about how to choose a career. The most important aspect of choosing your future job is finding one that fits your personality, suits your likes and dislikes, and provides a sense of fulfillment and satisfaction. This isn't a decision anyone else can make for you. Only *you* know what types of activities you like to do and what you don't, what fills you with a sense of excitement and challenge, and what makes you want to tear your hair out.

> **Don't do anything because everyone else thinks it's cool. Do something because YOU think it's cool.**
>
> —Seoung Hee, 16, Pennsylvania

To learn clues that will lead you to your ideal career, simply start paying attention to everything you do every day and cataloging in your mind the things you enjoy and the things you don't enjoy. Obviously everything you do may not relate to an actual job, but it will still give you an idea of how you feel about general types of work settings and tasks. Do you find yourself crabby and drained after spending a day with family or friends? Then you might prefer a job that allows you to work on your own at least part of the day. Do you enjoy solving problems required by a project that has been assigned for one of your classes? Then you might prefer a job that allows you to engage in similar creative or problem-solving tasks. Do you hate being supervised by others and doing routine or repetitive tasks? Then you might prefer a job that allows you plenty of autonomy, flexibility, and challenge. If you do this for even a few weeks or a month, you will be amazed at the knowledge you will accumulate about yourself—knowledge that will one day help you make that important career decision.

2. Wrong Way: Go for the money.

Right Way: Follow your heart. "Follow your bliss," said world-renowned mythologist Joseph Campbell. Doing what you love is one of the best ways of assuring that you will be successful. People who love what they do rarely fail at it, and people who hate what they do rarely succeed. Of course, there are always uncertainties in the economy and in the job market. But if you plan on being the best at whatever you decide to do, you will have more than enough job security. If you choose a career where the job openings are few, you must simply be more flexible in where you are willing to live, or be willing to accept a lower salary and take a second job while you establish yourself. But many people who opt for the lower-paying job they love do not regret their decision.

3. Wrong Way: Play it safe, since your opportunities are limited.

Right Way: Think out of the box. You are a powerful and talented being. Don't ever forget that. And you can change the world if you want to. Your career opportunities are virtually unlimited if you learn to problem-solve, think creatively, and challenge assumptions. Obviously, you will confront hurdles in your career if you make it your style to challenge and undercut others to make yourself look good. Teamwork is the word in the business world today. So if you act with integrity, treat others with respect, and speak up for yourself, you will succeed in whatever career you choose.

And if the corporate world doesn't offer you what you are looking for, be willing to go out on your own. Increasing numbers of women are successfully turning to self-employment. They're becoming entrepreneurs and starting their own businesses. They're working from home and working online. Be original. Find a way to make a living doing what you love—even if you have to invent a job for yourself.

4. Wrong Way: Choose now and stick with it.

Right Way: Take your time. Don't rush yourself to choose your future career—no matter how much pressure others may put on you to make a decision. Jumping into a career that isn't right for you almost assures a life of discontentment and frustration. It's worth the time it takes to make the right decision. If you get to college and still don't have any idea what you want to do, ask your college advisor if your college has a general studies degree. These are general programs of study that allow you to graduate with a college degree without necessarily honing in on a specific major.

In the process of earning the degree, you may discover something you really love and switch into that other major before graduation. Depending on how early you switch programs, you may take a little longer to graduate. But that's still better than deciding later in life that you hate what you do and need to go back to school for a whole new degree. Even if you don't find something you really like, you will still graduate with a college degree that will qualify you for many jobs. When you zero in on a career you want to pursue, don't hesitate to do whatever it takes to make the change. It's never too late to make the right career choice. Changing careers doesn't make everything you did up to that point a waste. Everything you have ever done contributes to your knowledge, wisdom, and skills.

5. Wrong Way: Choose only the "top hottest jobs."

Right Way: Talk to people in the field. Data and statistics don't tell you what you most need to know to decide whether a given career is right for you: what it's like working in that field. The only way to find this out is by talking to people with experience in that job. Try to find four or five people who have worked ten or more years in that career and interview them. Ask friends and family if they know anyone in that field. If they do, you have an in when you call for the interview.

If friends and family don't know anyone, you can just call local employers in the field and ask the receptionist to connect you with someone in the field you are researching. You'll be surprised at how helpful most people are when you tell them you are researching their career. If possible, make an appointment to come in to interview the person or, ideally, to "shadow" them (follow them around) on their job for a day or an afternoon. Get an internship, which is something common in college but that high school students also do. An internship is an unpaid job for which you might be able to get school credit.

❀ Fill Out a Job Application ❀

You're on the job hunt. Everywhere you go, you get handed that sheet of paper on a clipboard for you to fill out: the job application. Here's how to make yours stand out from the pile.

Lynda Orban also helps jobseekers find their perfect job on careerbuilder.com. She knows what to do when you're handed that sheet of paper:

Come prepared. When you go to fill out a job application, take the information you will need with you. These are things you might not have in your wallet, like a transcript from school, emergency contact info, and references (see the next section).

Have your references ready. Never list someone as a reference if you haven't talked to the person about it. The worst thing that could happen is that a potential employer calls a reference, and she says "Huh? Who?" or badmouths you. As you build experience in jobs, activities, and so on, get letters of recommendation. This will be helpful not only for jobs, but also for applying to colleges! Gather as you go. It'll be hard if you call someone and say, "Remember three years ago when I was in your Girl Scout troop? Can you write me a letter of recommendation?"

Handle the "experience" section. You might not have a ton of job experience, so you need to talk about school and extracurricular activities. Some of these might have the responsibilities of a "real" job. Talk about things like regular babysitting gigs, being treasurer of the Honors Society, volunteering, or being a member of a sports team.

Know your money facts. Most applications have a "wage desired" section. Don't just leave this blank. Don't ask for too little if you have great experience. But you have to have something to back you up for what you are asking. You have to start somewhere. Don't expect to make a ton at first.

Be honest. Bottom line: Be honest on your applications. Don't embellish, lie, and so forth, because the potential employer will find out.

Print neatly! Bring white-out. Sloppiness is a reflection on your professionalism.

◎ Get a Letter of Recommendation ◎

You're applying for a job.
You're getting your college application ready.
You're trying to get an internship.

You might need to get a letter of recommendation . . . or two . . . or three. You might be required to get the recommendation from a teacher, from another employer, or just from someone who knows you.

Helynna Brooke is the executive director of the San Francisco Mental Health Board. She's written many letters of recommendation, and has some advice on how to snag some good ones:

Choose someone who knows you, at least a little. Of course it's a good idea to choose someone who knows you a bit. Sometimes people get asked to write a recommendation for someone they hardly know. This is tricky because they not only might not know what to say, but they may not even be sure they want to recommend you.

Tell the person his or her opinion is valuable to you. When we want something like a recommendation, often we are nervous or uncomfortable because we're asking someone else for their comments or feelings about us. What we forget is that our request honors the person we are asking. We're saying to them that we value their opinion and who they are, that their recommendation is valuable.

And that's a good way to ask for a letter of recommendation: "I really have a lot of respect for you as a teacher and it would mean a lot to me if you would write me a recommendation for . . . (college/a job/whatever it is)."

Ask if you can help prepare the letter. Ask if the person would like you to write some of the things you would like to have highlighted in your recommendation letter. This may help them write it more easily and quickly. In fact, sometimes a person might respond to your request by asking you to write the letter for them. This is hard to do because it is hard for any of us to write a bragging letter about ourselves. When I've had to do that I usually sit down with a parent or really good friend and have that person help me.

Send a thank-you note. After a person agrees to write you a recommendation, send them a thank-you note. It can be just two sentences:

"Thank you so much for writing a letter of recommendation for me for _____. It meant a lot to me.

Sincerely, _____"

If you get into the college or get the job, send them a second quick note letting them know.

"I'm pleased to inform you that I got the _____ job for which I asked you to write a recommendation. I'm really excited and I start next week. Thank you again for your help."

You do this for two reasons:

1. If a person cares enough about you to do the recommendation, he or she will be interested in hearing about the outcome.

2. Very few people ever write notes, so you will really stand out—and standing out is especially helpful if you need to ask them again at a later time for another recommendation.

◎ Ace the Job Interview ◎

It's time to get a job! The first hurdle is exactly that, *getting* the job. And the most important step is the job interview.

One of my first job interviews was for a job at a Chuck E. Cheese restaurant. I remember the interview included putting on a giant rat costume and walking around the place. It was hot, and when I took off the rat head, I was sweaty and my hair was a static nightmare. I remember thinking: I'm not even applying for a costume job! I want to work at the candy counter or something. But I kept my sense of humor about it and smiled through the whole thing. It turned out to be a test to see my attitude. And trust me, you need to keep a good attitude when you are working in a place that caters to a thousand screaming little kids. Yup, I got the job.

(You know what? They took photos at that interview, where I had to dress up in that rat costume—with me holding the mask so you can see my face and know it's me, I guess for blackmail purposes. So somewhere out there, in the Chuck E. Cheese universe, there is a picture of me dressed like a sewer rat. I will give a hefty reward to anyone who returns that picture to me. No questions asked.)

Katharine Hansen is the author of several books for job hunters, including *A Foot in the Door: Networking Your Way into the Hidden Job Market*. Katharine knows that a job interview can be pretty nerve-wracking, so she wants to make it easier for you.

"As much as you'd like to be earning some money, the idea of job-hunting can be pretty intimidating. If you're feeling shy and lacking confidence about getting out there and talking to employers, you are far from alone, according to many career counselors."

Here are some tips from Katharine so you can ace the interview—and land the job!

Before the interview

Know yourself. Before you even start the job-hunting process, take some time to put yourself under the microscope. The more self-aware you are, the more comfortable and confident you will be in job interviews. Make a list of your strengths and abilities and another list of your achievements. Your accomplishments don't have to be spectacular. Your performance in school, extracurricular activities, jobs, and sports can all be indicators of a strong work ethic, leadership, teamwork, communication skills, and drive.

Know about the job for which you'll be interviewing. Be sure to carefully read and understand the job description. Think about yourself in relation to the job. Then ask yourself, "What do I have that would make someone want to hire me for this job?"

Understand what employers are looking for. Employers hiring teens are often concerned with reliability issues. Some teen employees are chronically late to work, don't show up at all, or constantly ask for schedule changes to accommodate other activities. Thus, you need to reassure the employer that these typical teen problems won't be a problem with you, and give examples based on your past performance.

Practice. Ask friends and family members to conduct practice interviews with you. You can find many lists of commonly asked interview questions on the Internet or in interviewing books. Also practice your body language (see page 15!) and handshake (see page 78!).

Be prepared to be interviewed even when you're not expecting it. If you're cruising the mall filling out job applications, don't be surprised if some employers want to interview you on the spot. The nature of the jobs that teens typically seek makes impromptu interviews more likely than for other age groups, and they are especially likely if the store has a "Help Wanted" sign in the window. Since you could be interviewed at any time, you should dress appropriately when you go out to fill out applications. Also be mentally prepared, and don't say no if an employer asks to interview you on the spot.

Have realistic expectations about salary. Let's face it; most teen jobs pay minimum wage. Know what the current minimum wage is. If the situation seems right, you could even consider asking for more. You could make a case for your ability to do a better job than those who receive minimum wage. Be careful here, though; being too pushy about salary could cost you the job.

Know what hours you can work, and prepare to be flexible. Consider school, homework, extracurricular activities, sports—anything that takes up your time. Be able to clearly articulate to the employer the hours you are available to work. If the employer needs more availability, and you really want the job, consider giving up a nonessential activity.

Dress appropriately! (See page 52.)

At the interview

Arrive on time. Punctuality and reliability are a matter of show and tell.

You can show your punctuality by arriving 5 to 15 minutes early for the interview. But you can also tell about your punctuality and reliability based on your performance in previous jobs and school.

Don't downplay your previous experience, no matter how lowly it seems. Babysitting, delivering papers, mowing lawns, and similar jobs are all worthwhile because they enabled you to use transferable skills. You can point to traits and skills gained, such as reliability, responsibility, flexibility, punctuality, and interpersonal skills.

Make eye contact. It's extremely important for connecting with your interviewer. When asked a question, don't look up at the walls and ceiling as if searching for answers. Don't cast your eyes downward. One expert, recognizing that eye contact is hard to maintain in a one-on-one situation, says to look at the interviewer's nose.

Be yourself. Don't be afraid to open a window into your personality and interject some humor into the interview.

Show your enthusiasm. Employers list lack of enthusiasm as their number one turnoff in interviewees. The best way to show enthusiasm? Smile frequently throughout the interview.

Exude confidence. Among the best ways to show confidence are a strong, forceful voice and clear enunciation. No matter how shaky you may feel inside, try your best to show a confident attitude.

Ask questions. Interviewers almost always invite you to ask questions at the end of the interview. Asking questions shows your enthusiasm for the job, so have a couple prepared, but don't ask about things like salary or vacation time. Some good questions to ask include:

* Can you describe a typical day for someone in this position?
* What is the top priority of the person who accepts this job?
* Why did you come to work here? What keeps you here?

Close the sale. If you want the job, say so. Conclude the interview with a statement that conveys your enthusiasm for the position. You could also ask if the interviewer has any questions about your ability to do the job. If the interviewer expresses any reservations, you can address them and try to ease the employer's concerns. Find out when the company plans to make its hiring decision and whether they will contact you either way. Be sure to smile, thank the interviewer, and extend your hand for an exit handshake.

After the interview

Write a thank-you note. It's just common courtesy to thank people for their time, and since very few teens exercise this little gesture, you'll stand out if you do it. If the interviewer has a business card, ask for one to ensure that you spell his or her name correctly.

Step-by-Step:
Walking into the Interview

- When you walk into an interview, remain standing until asked to be seated. Have confident posture. Stand straight, sit properly. If the person interviewing you does not offer a seat, ask where you should sit. Don't take over by sitting before asked.

- If you bring a briefcase or purse, don't put it on someone's desk; leave it beside your chair.

- Turn your cell phone off before you arrive.

- Shake hands when you first walk in. Introduce yourself. Make eye contact and smile. Don't fidget. Sit up straight; don't lean on the desk or table.

Ready? . . . Go!

—Nicole DeVault is an etiquette expert.

If you haven't heard a hiring decision by the time you expected to, call the interviewer to check on your status. Don't make a pest of yourself, but do follow up.

Did you get the job? If you did, congratulate yourself. It isn't always an easy task. If you didn't, think about reasons they didn't hire you. Sometimes things are out of your control, like the owner's daughter decided she wanted it instead, or you just didn't have the right qualifications. But if you think you might have botched it, reread the above suggestions. If they call to reject you, you might even ask them politely if they have any suggestions for your improvement. And don't feel terrible; just about every single person has been turned down for a job at some time or another. Keep on applying and trying.

✖ Get Work Experience ✖

Every hour of work experience you have helps you learn something that will pay off in your work future. Even my first "real" job at Burger King taught me something: how to handle money (cash register), how to stay cool around people who are being total jerks ("Hey girly, I said extra ketchup—you call this *extra ketchup?!?!*"), and that I never EVER wanted to work somewhere that I had to wear a polyester brown and yellow uniform again.

But really, even the smallest of jobs you have *now* can help you along in the future—more than you know!

"It's never too early to begin preparing yourself for your career," says Maria Bailey, author of *The Woman's Home-Based Business Book of Answers* and founder and CEO of BlueSuitMom.com. "Even if you haven't decided what profession you'll pursue, preparing yourself for making a living is a smart strategy for life."

So can you find the right opportunities to prepare yourself for a career you've yet to identify? It is not as much about the experience of a particular job. It's in the characteristics you demonstrate. No matter what career you decide to pursue later, employers look for these elements of work ethic in any employee they hire:

- Responsibility
- Dedication
- Willingness to learn
- Good attitude
- Loyalty

And you can work in many ways to cultivate these characteristics. And then show in your résumé that you possess them. The easiest way to demonstrate your work ethic is this: work! This can either be through volunteer work or paid work.

Get work as a volunteer or intern. You don't have to be paid to get work experience. Don't count out volunteer work as an important experience in preparing yourself for your profession.

See the section on Volunteering (page 197) for more information.

Get a paid job. A paid job also offers an opportunity to demonstrate your determination to work. Because you're earning money, it also tells future employers that you respect money and have the desire to work hard for it.

Although it's always nice to get job experience in a field you hope to one day pursue, it isn't always necessary. From babysitting to working on a construction site, life-guarding to scooping ice cream—all experience counts. A part-time position at Wendy's demonstrates a strong work ethic as much as a part-time position at a prestigious law firm—as long as you work hard and win the respect of your employer. You may just think of making burgers at Wendy's as a good way to earn some extra spending money, but it offers more to your résumé. It shows that you have experience working with a major consumer brand, you learned to multi-task, handle a paycheck, and manage your time well at an early age. It shows a high degree of responsibility to juggle schoolwork and a job.

It is never too early to begin to prepare for the future. A strong résumé will follow you for a long time.

> Always be on your best behavior because you never know who is watching. The stranger on the street may be your future boss or your next boyfriend's parents!
>
> —Jillian, 13, Ohio

◇ Quit Gracefully ◇

Time to leave! Time to move on! You're quitting your job. Maybe you had a great experience. Then you're probably nervous and sad about telling your boss you're leaving. Maybe the experience, well, wasn't so hot, and you're dying to say "I'm outta here, you jerk, and I hope I never see this stupid place again!" and to slam the door on the way out.

Um, that last one is not recommended. Hold yourself back. And listen to Timi Gleason, an executive and career coach who used to be a human resources director (so she knows a lot about hiring and firing). Here's how to quit with style, grace, and a sense of professionalism.

Tell your supervisor first. Would you want to hear important news through the grapevine? No. You want to be kept in the loop. Bosses want to be treated supportively, too.

Either hand your boss a note as you tell him or her that you are giving two weeks notice, or pull him aside, "Jerry, can you give me two minutes? I need to update you on something important. I'm going to have to quit (or resign) my job here (insert a reason if you want to). I don't want to put you in a tight spot for help so I am giving you notice. Would you like two weeks, or can you find someone to replace me sooner?"

Just figure your boss may be concerned and disappointed about having to replace you, and be ready to treat him with respect and maturity. You'd be surprised how bosses feel when they lose an employee and have only a short period of time to find another.

Give a reason for leaving. Do this if you are quitting for reasons other than you hate it there, such as: ". . . to a better paying job," ". . . for advancement purposes," or ". . . to move to another area to attend school or be with family."

Give two weeks' notice. It is standard practice to give two weeks' notice to employers before you leave. This gives them time to find someone else to replace you. Consider the fact that they will have to put an ad in the newspaper on a weekend, and then interview and select someone.

Give a letter of resignation. The letter only needs to be one to three sentences stating your intentions, including the date of your last workday. Be courteous and professional in the letter. Be sure to put a date on the letter and to keep track of conversations and the dates that follow your resignation. Keep a copy of letters. Give letters to bosses in person or to their assistant. Leaving resignation letters on a desk isn't a fair or a dependable system. If you give your employer two weeks' notice and she lets you go early, you may be eligible for unemployment insurance under some circumstances.

Always quit a job if you are not being treated appropriately. If you're not sure, talk to a professional person (parents, guidance counselor, any human resource manager, clergy, older businessperson) who can verify your concerns. That includes requests or hints for sexual favors, physical abuse, verbal abuse, not getting paid on time, illegal drugs or property being sold through the business, your being used to commit illegal transactions, and so on.

Make arrangements to collect your last paycheck. In most states, employers owe you your paycheck within 72 hours of quitting. If you give two weeks' notice (or more than 72 hours notice), they owe you your check at the time you leave.

Don't burn bridges. This means forget the "I'm outta here, you jerk, and I hope I never see this stupid place again!" (Door slam!) Do the right thing. Protect yourself by creating a simple paper trail, and don't lose your cool. (This is probably one of those times you may not want to work an additional two weeks, but before you decide to leave them high and dry, see if you can work it out peacefully.)

When you quit a job, consider the fact that a future employer might ask you why you left it. And they may check with your old boss to ask whether your reason is accurate. But often, they are only looking for a good answer that makes sense and indicates that you were being responsible to your previous company.

❖ Budget Your Money ❖

You've got some money coming in! You're babysitting. You're selling bracelets you make. You have a part-time job. You've got your allowance. And the money is all yours. Money, money, MONEY! YEAH!

Stick It Out

Try to stay at each job for six months or more (unless it's a seasonal job) to show your ability to be stable (a committed employee) and to demonstrate that you were desirable (they kept you on because you were doing a good job).

Sorry, don't run to the mall quite yet. First it's time to learn how to manage your money.

Why *should* you learn to manage your money now? I mean, you might be thinking, "I have the rest of my adult life to deal with that." Or, "I really don't make enough money now to worry about it." Or, "That's for my parents to take care of."

Not true.

Marilyn Hall is a personal coach. One of the skills she coaches people on is managing their money.

The key skills you want to learn include:

- Saving money
- Keeping track of where your money comes from and where it goes
- Observing the flow of money in your life
- Enjoying the process of seeing your savings grow and your worth increase

Marilyn has a system for you to follow so you can do it!

Step 1: Track where your money comes from, how much comes in, and where it all goes.

This will give you a wealth of information that will allow you to see how you're spending this important symbol of your success.

How? Make a Money Notebook. Use a loose-leaf binder with some tabs and paper. For the next week or two, record all the money that comes to you, and everything you spend it on.

After that is done, you have a recorded history of your spending. Label these expenditures into three categories:

- *Fun and Games:* Things like candy, sodas, movies, go-cart rides, and eating out. These items represent the things you do purely for fun that tend to occur frequently, and involve relatively small amounts of money.

- *Necessary Items:* These are things you must pay for that you require, like books, uniforms, equipment, or an overdue library fine.

- *Big and Important Items:* This might be a prom dress, an airline ticket to visit a friend, a canoe trip, speed skates, or a new tennis racket. These expenses involve a fairly large amount of money and usually can't be purchased from just one week's earnings. It is often necessary to save for a period of time to afford these expenditures.

Step 2: Decide where to put your money.

Divide your money into three individual places as soon as you receive it. Call them: *Petty Cash, Specific Savings,* and *Golden Savings.*

- *Petty Cash* will be the fund you draw from to pay for items in the *Fun and Games* expenses from Step 1, and for some of the smaller *Necessary Items.* This fund is for short-term expenses that tend to recur.

- *Specific Savings* is where you save up money for the big-ticket items you wish to purchase. All of your *Big and Important* purchases will come from here, and some of the *Necessary Items* that cost more.

- *Golden Savings* is something you can take pride in for years to come. This is the portion of your money that is put away in a safe place, which you don't intend to touch for a long, long time. But you can watch it, observe its growth, and celebrate it as an important part of your present and future wealth.

Decide on a physical space to put each of these funds. *Petty Cash* should be kept in a safe but accessible place, perhaps hidden in your room. If you have a checking account, *Specific Savings* can be kept there, or perhaps in a savings account, where it can earn interest until you use it. Your *Golden Savings* will be kept in an interest-bearing savings account.

Now let's see a picture of how your money will flow with this new system:

1. <u>Money comes in</u>	2. <u>Divide into funds</u>	3. <u>Pay expenses</u>
	Petty Cash	Fun and Games
	Specific Savings	Necessary Items
	Golden Savings	Big and Important

So when your money is received, the first thing you'll do is divide it between the three funds. Then, you will pull from the *Petty Cash* and *Specific Savings* funds to pay for your expenses and purchases. *Golden Savings* is considered "untouchable"—but don't let that stop you from enjoying how it is growing!

Step 3: Make your personal money plan.

You now have some very powerful tools. With the funds you have established, the categories for your expenses and purchases, as well as your desires for your wealth and success . . . you can begin to shape your future!

First, plan your Golden Savings. This is the most important step, which will impact your financial status greatly. Do not make the mistake of determining your contribution to Golden Savings after you have decided how much to spend on fun and necessary things. Keep the growth of this fund your highest priority, and you will be on a path to creating a steady stream of wealth and prosperity in your life.

It may be tough to determine a set amount to contribute to Golden Savings each month. Much of your income is disposable, meaning you probably do not have huge obligations like a mortgage on a house. It may also be variable—that is, its amount changes, depending on different jobs and your availability to do them.

Therefore, consider establishing a percentage of your ongoing income to put into this long-term savings category. Start out fairly aggressively—how about 50 percent? Could you still afford your other expenses if you saved half of what you bring in? If so, go for it. If not, then scale back—but don't drop below 30 percent!

Once you have determined what to put into Golden Savings, the rest must be divided between Petty Cash and Specific Savings. To do this, look closely at your previously tracked expenses in *Fun and Games, Necessary Items,* and *Big and Important.*

Ask some important questions here. Are these expenses predictable? Which ones tend to recur? Do you spend a similar amount in each category each month? What about at different times of the year? Do you see patterns in your spending that enable you to plan? Do you often "come up short" and have to ask your parents or somebody else to bail you out? All of this information is helpful as you do your planning.

The answers to these questions will help you make key decisions about your Petty Cash and Specific Savings funds. Will it make sense to contribute only what you think you will need to each fund, or keep it a bit "padded"? Can you find ways to cut back on expenses in one area so more money will be available for another fund? Make adjustments as needed, either to the amounts in these two funds or in your spending, so that the shortfalls are few and far between.

Step 4: Put the plan into action.

The money comes in? Follow your plan.

Record your notes, thoughts, and changes in your Money Notebook. As you continue to work with your budgeting and saving program, customize it as your income, expenses, and circumstances change. Have fun with it! Be ever sensitive to the flow of your income. And always, always give your wonderful Golden Savings the highest priority in your money decisions!

Ta-da! If you do this, you will be ahead of the game (more so than many adults!). Now is a great time to learn how to put money aside on a regular basis to create ongoing wealth and prosperity in your life. Develop this powerful "saving habit" now, and you will be strong, informed, and in a position to make good decisions for years to come.

✥ Do Fads—to a Point ✥

It's spring! Those new sandals are so in! And those sunglasses—fresh! You've got to run out to the mall and fill your closet with all the latest and greatest!

You got your allowance. And you're ready to spend it on the newest stuffed beanbag for your collection. Someday you're going to make a ton selling it when they're collector's items!

First day of school. Oh—everyone who matters is wearing *that* brand of shoes. You better hit the shoe store, right?

You're faced with fads every day. They're not a bad thing. (This is not a lecture, here!) Fads and being trendy can be fun . . .

. . . to a point.

Jayne Pearl is the author of *Kids and Money: Giving Them the Savvy to Succeed Financially* and a business writer for major financial magazines, radio shows, and on Oxygen.com. Jayne says:

> We're all fed into the cycle of constant consumption. We see thousands of ads a day, on TV, radio, and the Internet; on the bus; even on other people's clothes. We feel like we have to buy, buy, buy. Have everything. We're all guilty of falling for it sometimes. Think about it. You've got pressure from friends and school where you have to wear the right labels, have the right items. But it doesn't mean you have to follow it *blindly*.
>
> First, understand that there is a huge amount of money being spent trying to influence teens. Companies work very hard trying to make you think things are cool so you will spend your money on them, which makes more money for them.
>
> Teens often think that they create the trends and it's their peer group that is determining what's cool. But that isn't true. There are companies that make a lot of money trying to spot trends and then feeding the trends to companies so they can be part of it. There are "cool hunters," hip young people whose job is to calculate every twitch teens make.
>
> For example, the company's cool hunters discover what new clothing looks are popping up on the streets. They feed

the information to their client, a major clothing company. The client manufactures clothes based on that information and sells them in their teen stores. And then all sorts of ads try to convince you that you will find love, your friends will like you, and you will be happy *only* if you have that item.

Doesn't that make you feel manipulated?

It should! Teens are being seriously manipulated and need to know it, so they can make conscious decisions. It's important to understand trends so you can make your own decisions. And then, you still might want to buy a product! But at least you'll be making a conscious decision.

So how do you do that?! Jayne says:

Know the difference between needs and wants. Think about your needs versus wants. Needs are what you need to survive: food, shelter, some clothing to protect you from the elements. Wants are, well, things you want: a particular brand of food, the latest fashions. Sometimes it seems like you've just *got* to have that jacket or else. But take a second and realize that you don't *need* it. There's nothing wrong with material things and enjoying the fruits of your work. But you need to understand you don't *need* most of the stuff you *want*.

Ask yourself why you want it. Why do you want the item? Because you have so much fun with it? It looks great on you? Makes you feel happy?

Or do you want the item because everyone else has one and it just seems like you should, too? If you buy something just to fit in, at least admit to yourself that is the reason you are doing it. Once you start admitting that to yourself, it will help you be more discriminating about what you buy. It's okay to follow the pack to an extent, but not if that's the only way you can feel good about yourself.

Take a reality check. Say everyone has the product now, but you just can't afford it. Should you take a second job, beg your parents, do what it takes to get it?

First, put things in perspective. Go to your closet. Haul out stuff from last year you just *had* to have at the time. Stuff you don't use. Ask yourself: How much did it cost? How long did you stay interested in it? How did it hold up?

Was it worth it? A lot of the times, your answer will be NO. Is that likely to happen with this new product?

Be selective. Being cool doesn't mean running out and grabbing up every fad that comes along. Then you're just a blind follower, not a leader. Choose a few fads that make you feel happy and special. And let the others go.

Wait a month. Wait six months. Wait as long as you can stand it.

When a fad is at its peak, the stores can charge more. Later, it chills out a bit. You can save a fortune after the prices go down. And by then, you also might not want it anymore.

There are always ways to "buy into" a fad inexpensively. If a certain shade of green is all the craze one season, find a hair scrunchie or a scarf in that color and spend just a few dollars instead of $50 on a sweater that color.

Use fads in a conscious way. If you've gone through this list, and you still think it empowers you to have the item, then go ahead and give it a try. That's the right reason to buy into a fad.

⚙ Be an Entrepreneur ⚙

When I was five, my twin sister and I started our first business. We caught these huge crickets in the woods by our house and put them in a box. We then went around the neighborhood door to door, asking people if they wanted to buy a cricket for a nickel. We had some success; other kids bought a few.

But we ran into a couple snags. A lot of moms answered the door and were grossed out—especially when we would open the box to show them what we had and a bunch of crickets would jump out and make a break for freedom. And then the fatal flaw: We didn't realize you should poke holes in the lid. So we had to have a mass burial of our product. We learned some business lessons that day. And felt a little guilty about our profits since they were at the expense of the poor crickets.

Have *you* ever dreamed of starting your own business? Elizabeth Carlassare wrote a book called *DotCom Divas* and interviewed a bunch of successful women Internet entrepreneurs. Elizabeth says this:

> Many young women and, yes, even girls have started their own successful businesses. Starting your own business can be incredibly satisfying and allows you to directly reap the rewards of your own efforts. Starting your own business doesn't need to be a big production. There are many ways to start small and test the waters to see if entrepreneurship might be for you.

Is entrepreneurship for you?

By now, you may be thinking that starting your own business sounds fun and exciting—and profitable. But how do you tell if entrepreneurship is really for you? Entrepreneurs tend to have some characteristics in common. See whether *you* have what it takes:

* Are you adept at spotting opportunities?
* Are you passionate and enthusiastic?
* Are you persistent?
* Are you a people person and a good communicator?
* Are you optimistic?
* Do you enjoy being independent?
* Are you a hard worker?

If you answered "yes" to most of these seven questions, you share the key personality traits of successful entrepreneurs.

Here are ways to get started.

Focus on something you are good at and that you enjoy. What do you do well? What do you like to do? You're most likely to be successful if your business lets you do something you enjoy and capitalizes on your talents. Make a list of all the things you enjoy doing and are good at. Maybe you have a talent for playing the flute, entertaining children, or repairing bicycles. Are there business opportunities in any of the things on your list?

Look for an unfilled need. When you're keeping your eyes open for a business idea, keep your mind open, too. You never know when you'll discover a need that hasn't yet been filled. Pay attention when someone has a problem or frustration. There could be a business opportunity in solving it. For example, if you hear your neighbors complaining because their yards are full of weeds, you could offer to weed it for them. Or, if you notice that your neighbors work and they have a dog, you could start a dog-walking service and approach them to be your first customer.

Start small and keep it simple. It's a good idea to start your business in a small way at first to test it out and see if you like it. If you think you might enjoy babysitting, try it a few times. If all goes well, start spreading the word. If you're good at math, try tutoring a student who needs some math help. See how it goes, and if you decide to grow your business, you can put the word out.

And, if you start a business and find you don't enjoy it or aren't able to make any money with it, remember that it's okay to walk away from it and try something else. Many successful entrepreneurs have experienced business failures before going on to create profitable enterprises. (Like my dead cricket store. Yuk.)

◎ Be a Model—or Not ◎

So you want to be a model. Lots of girls do, and some even become models. Many more girls get sucked into scams. They listen to people who promise to make them a star, but those people just take their money . . . or worse.

Cheli Cerra has been a model for designers like Calvin Klein. She has heard it all. She remembers when she was a teen, people would always ask her, "Are you a model?" She wanted to be one but didn't know how. First, weed out the scams. And Cheli tells you how:

Fortunately for me, a family friend who was already modeling showed me the ropes and told me what to do. She also told me what to watch out for and I will gladly share this with you.

One common and dangerous scam is to be approached off the street. A man (or woman) approaches you and asks if you are a model. He claims to be a photographer and gives you his card. He says he wants to shoot some pictures of you. He has connections. He can make you a star. Don't fall for it. Keep walking. Never take off with a stranger who approaches you; this is the older version of what you learned to refuse when you were little: "Little girl, do you want some candy?"

Suppose the "photographer" says there is a modeling shoot right now and you need to go with him right away. DO NOT go. Any professional photographer and professional modeling agency plans ahead for their fashion shoots.

Here is more advice from Cheli:

- **Never go to a photo shoot alone.** The best thing to do is bring a parent or adult.

- **Never let a photographer talk you into something you don't want to do.** This includes taking off your clothes or having something to drink (in case it is drugged).

- **Don't pay a huge amount of money to get your photo taken.** Some photographers claim in their ads that they will guarantee you a modeling job. First, you have to get your photos taken with them and pay them a couple thousand dollars. Hold it right there. A reputable professional photographer will not charge this price for modeling pictures. When shooting with a photographer for the first time, always check them out by asking for references.

- **Don't believe that you have to take off your clothes to get a legitimate modeling job.** Legitimate modeling agencies don't accept nude or pornographic photos. A photographer who tells you otherwise and asks you to do a lingerie, swimsuit, or nude shoot only wants to get you out of your clothes.

- **Don't go to a modeling agency that advertises that you can "Become a model for $500" or another certain amount of money.** Legitimate modeling agencies do not ask for a modeling fee to see you and evaluate your modeling potential.

Are you a makeup freak? When your friends come over, do they end up with a total face makeover? Have you ever dreamed of creating your own makeup? Was the giant Barbie makeup head your favorite toy? Galit Strugano was only 23 when she founded girLActik, a sparkly makeup line worn by celebrities like Destiny's Child, Julia Roberts, Britney Spears, Eden's Crush, and the *NSYNC dancers. Galit gives advice on how to break into a competitive field with a small amount of savings and a big idea:

- Experiment with makeup.

- Try out your makeup ideas. On friends, do makeup for events for free.

- Keep up with what is hot. Read fashion and teen magazines and Web sites.

- Distinguish yourself from everyone else. The cosmetics industry is so competitive, especially in the trend area. Create something that is unique. My first product was a sparkly makeup base. Find something that doesn't exist and create it.

- Find a trustworthy chemist.

- Come up with a great name. The first name I chose was Galactic, but that was taken. My line is a "girly thing," so I named it girLActik. The L and A are capitalized because it originated in L.A. I also use the word "sparkly," and not "glitter."

- Have a motto. Mine is, "Be a star and feel like a star."

- **Don't sign anything you don't understand or haven't read.** If you are a minor, you'll need at least one parent's signature. If you aren't a minor, still let your parents and possibly

How to Find a Modeling Agency

1. Find agencies that have SAG (Screen Actors Guild) affiliation.

2. Ask questions about the modeling agency that you are interested in: Ask about references and for a client list.

3. Many legitimate modeling agencies have a day during the week called "open call days." Find out what day the agency you are interested in has this. Go prepared. An open call day is a day that the agency sees new talent. Take along a couple of pictures of yourself. These can be pictures that your family has taken of you; they do not have to be professionally done. If an agency is genuinely interested in you, they will send you to various photographers to "test" (get pictures) at a minimum cost to begin to build your portfolio. If you feel that you really want to take a professionally done picture, have an 8-by-10 head shot done and take this with you to the open call day.

4. Check out the Modeling Association of America (MAAI), a nonprofit organization. Find it on the Internet at www.maai.org.

a lawyer take a second look. If it's legitimate, it can't hurt to have them check it out.

• **Watch out for Internet modeling agencies.** Know who the company you are working with is. Find the answers to these questions: Do they have a street address? Do they have a section that tells you what they do with your personal information? Is there a privacy statement? Is there a person listed as a contact with a legitimate phone number, not a cell phone? Legitimate modeling agencies use the Internet as a tool but have "brick and mortar" places of business. If you

USE COMMON SENSE! The modeling business is full of con artists, greedy people who want to make money off of you. Never pay "up front" for pictures. Be wary of talent searches. If it sounds too good to be true, it probably isn't true.

have any doubts, call the Better Business Bureau or check them online. Many states have laws and these laws make agencies hold state licenses.

◎ Talk Sports ◎

Hey, did you see the game last night?

Have you ever been standing with a group of people—okay, usually guys—and they're all jabbering about the latest sports: who won, who stinks, how "their" team is doing. This is how guys naturally bond with each other. But sports talk is so not just for guys. You probably know girls who can out–sports talk guys. My sister Amy is like that. Go ahead: Quiz her. Ask her who's playing, the stats, whatever. She knows them.

When you don't know how to talk sports, you get left out. And why be left out? Say you're scooping ice cream at work, and your manager comes in and says, "Hey, how about those Mets?" George, the scooper next to you, starts a conversation with your manager about stats and teams and players. You have nothing to say. Manager gives George some high fives and pretty much disregards you.

But hey, don't learn something just to be part of the crowd. Another reason to learn to talk sports is just that it can be f-u-n. Here's how. Andrea LaPlante is the affiliate relations manager at Fox Sports Net. She can help you talk sports with the best of 'em—or at least enough so you can hold your own.

Keep up with what's hot and what's not in the world of sports. Every sport has its season. Focus on the sport of the moment.

When it's basketball season, at least pay attention during tournament time. When it's baseball season, keep up during the playoffs. During the Olympics, you've got a ton to choose from.

> If someone doesn't like you for who you are, then that person isn't worth your time.
>
> —Patricia, 18, Massachusetts

Watch the game. This may seem obvious, but I suggest that in order to know what's going on, watching the game is the best way to know. Go to a game or watch it on television. The best way to get excited and carry on a conversation about a game is if you watched it.

Know the lingo. Make sure to understand the terms used in games. As a woman, it is best to be educated when discussing sports. You lose credibility when all you can talk about is the color of the uniforms or how cute the quarterback is. Make sure you understand the fundamentals of the game (points, time-outs, quarters, touchdown, fouls, offense, defense, and so on).

Know the heavy hitters. Pick out a few major league players on your favorite teams. Make sure to know the big names and how they're doing this season. It's more fun to talk about someone you know.

Take up golf. This one's going to help you later in the business world. So much business is done on the golf course. Golfers love to talk golf and you can bond with a client when you can talk golf with him or her. Building relationships is key to retaining and growing business. When you can spend a day golfing with a client, you have their undivided attention.

Place a bet. I am not advocating serious gambling, but I do believe that placing a bet with friends or family during tournament time makes it a heck of a lot more interesting. Say it is March Madness (college basketball's hot time). You don't even have to know anything about the teams in the college basketball tournament, but the best part about the final four is pulling out your picks and watching the upsets. You can place small bets on championship games to keep them interesting. It doesn't have to be money; you can bet doing the dishes or something.

Have a sports buddy. It's so much fun calling up a friend after watching a great sporting event and reliving the details together. The excitement and memories you create with your friend will push you to keep watching.

Get expert advice. Have someone you can call for a quick review of the latest and greatest. It's like having your own personal cheat sheet. It could be a family member, the newspaper, or the Internet.

Go to a game and have fun. The reason people buy season tickets and paint their faces is because it is *fun!* All these years, men have dominated sports conversations and have been the ones who most often go to the games. The reason for this, we all know, is because men are big kids. When was the last time you went to a sporting event? You grab some obnoxious food and get to paint your face and scream and yell; and if your team wins, you get to jump up and down.

Be passionate about sports. When all is said and done, have passion for your favorite player or team. You can make an instant connection with a stranger over the discussion of your favorite player or team. Everyone can relate to the feeling of being a "fan."

MY TEAMS:

The Yankees!

The Buffalo Bills!

Ohio State! Go Bucks!

Go! Go! Go!

※ Move Your Body ※

Working out. Playing sports. Just . . . moving!

Gun Denhart is always on the move. She even attributes some of her success to staying physically active. And she has had a lot of success as the co-founder of Hanna Andersson, a really successful catalog company, and is now the chairperson of the Hanna Andersson Charitable Foundation, an organization that funds groups benefiting needy children and women. Gun says:

> I grew up in Sweden. Physical education was an important part of school. I was always doing some kind of physical activity. I still do. But here in America, I see that physical education gets lost in the shuffle. When my son was in high school here, he didn't even have P.E.
>
> But to have a healthy mind, you have to have a healthy body. You've got to move your body to feel good. There have been times where I felt I didn't have time to exercise. When I started my company I was so busy that I didn't consider it a priority. And I felt awful. When I am physically active, I have more energy and I'm in so much better shape.

Here are Gun's suggestions for you:

Don't feel you have to compete. The American culture is focused on competitive sports. But if you don't want to be on a sports team, don't think you can't be physical. You don't even have to be particularly good at it. Take long walks, or put on some music and dance around the room (you might want to pull down the blinds).

Sweat. To get the benefits of physical activity, you need to get your heart rate up for at least 20 minutes, three times a week. Get sweaty!

Try exercising outdoors. Exercising outdoors is a great stress reliever. Being out in the fresh air is also good for your skin. Go for a hike, play tennis, ski cross country, jog.

Try new activities and see if you like them. I discovered yoga, and it has become my passion.

◈ Think Like an Athlete ◈

Do you consider yourself an athlete? If yes, read on. If no, read on anyway—and find out why you should start thinking like one to set yourself up for success.

How can you pick the right sport for you? Donna Lopiano is the president of the Women's Sports Foundation. (The Web site, womenssportsfoundation.org, has a section for girls' sports called Go Girl Go!) Donna says:

> The reason people participate in sports is because it is fun, not to win gold medals and get paid a million dollars. Sports are not fun unless you have success. Success directly relates to skills, which directly relates to body size, weight, and flexibility. There are over 100 different sports, and more than one meets your requirements, physique, and time restrictions. You shouldn't break your back trying to do something you're not going to be good at.

Here are some ideas for finding the right sport for you.

1. **Time:** How long does the sport take to play?

2. **Ease of learning:** Does it take an afternoon to learn, or years to learn?

3. **Commitment:** How dedicated can you be?

4. **Equipment cost:** Can you afford this sport? Are startup costs high but maintenance costs low (hint, Mom and Dad, my birthday is coming up!)?

5. **Injury risk:** Is track your true passion but you want something for the off-season? Look for a low-risk sport so you don't jeopardize your true love.

6. **Endurance, strength, and skill required:** If you work best in short bursts of energy, look for low-endurance sports.

7. **Access to facilities:** Will you spend half the time just looking for somewhere to play?

Mariah Burton Nelson has been a professional basketball player and a sportswriter, as well as an author. Her story is very inspiring. She faced boundaries as a female athlete, when those two words were not often linked together. Mariah tells how the lessons she learned playing sports helped her take risks and make her dreams come true:

> I wanted to be an author. I loved reading and writing, and that seemed like the most marvelous thing in the world: to write my own book.
>
> But when I was 4, I wrote a story and showed it to my big brother Peter, who was two years older. He promptly intimidated me.
>
> "You did it wrong," he said.
>
> I have since learned not to take anything the critics say too seriously—especially if they're only 6 years old. I've also learned not to listen to anyone who just might feel jealous of my talents! But as a kid, I was crushed.
>
> Later a teacher discouraged me by saying, "Okay, you want to be an author, but what are you going to do for a living? Fewer than 5 percent of all writers make a living at it."
>
> After I retired from basketball, I remembered my writing dream. At 24, my life seemed to be going by quickly. I wondered, "Am I going to wake up one day and say, 'Uh-oh, I'm 84 years old, and I always wanted to be a writer, but was afraid to try'?"
>
> I thought about everything I'd learned in sports. Might any of these skills come in handy, I wondered, if I pursued becoming an author?
>
> Now—many years later—I have accomplished my childhood dream of becoming an author, and have written four books (so far!). I've written hundreds of articles for the biggest newspapers. I still practice, writing almost every day. I still have coaches (writing mentors) and teammates (friends and colleagues who want me to succeed). When I receive rejection notices, I'm disappointed; but I draw on my athletic experience to remember that athletes don't quit when they lose.
>
> Are you an athlete? Try claiming that identity. You don't have to be a pro. You don't even have to be on a junior varsity team. You just have to approach the world with an athletic sort of attitude, using lessons from the playing fields to

help you reach your goals, as I did. Here's how I define it: An athlete is someone who enjoys challenges; practices physical and mental skills with a goal in mind; and plays well with others.

Here are Mariah's suggestions for ways to think like an athlete:

Enjoy challenges. Welcome adversity, saying "yes" when an opportunity to excel comes your way. Welcome pressure, too, using that pressure to help you rise to your best level of performance, on or off the playing fields. This is what athletes call getting psyched up (and non-athletes call being nervous, scared, or terrified!).

Practice physical and mental skills with a goal in mind. Discipline your body and mind by rehearsing success—toward a particular goal. Whether you're playing softball, playing the piano, or playing around with a computer program you're trying to master, practice isn't always fun, but it *can* be fun—and in any case it's required for success. There's really no other way.

Play well with others. Even individual-sport athletes (skaters, swimmers, skiers) and professionals in solitary pursuits (like writing) must respect and cooperate with teachers, coaches, teammates, officials, family members, and friends. Athletes focus on their own goals, but are also kind, helpful, and grateful to other people in their lives. Life is a team sport.

Think of yourself as an athlete. Act like an athlete. Pursue your goals using athletic principles like teamwork, practice, and persistence. I guarantee you this will change the way you stand, the way you walk, the goals you set for yourself, and the dreams you make come true.

☼ Be Stronger ☼

Yup, physically stronger. Remember, no helpless females here! Being strong helps you be empowered. If you're strong, you can be a better athlete. You can be more independent. Hey, you need to be strong just to lug your backpack full of books around school!

Kathy Roberts is one of the strongest women in the world. She is a power lifter who holds world and American records in Lifetime Drug-Free weight classes. Kathy says that it's very important for teen girls to be strong physically as well as mentally and emotionally. Kathy says that some girls are born naturally strong, while others may have strength in them but don't even know that it exists. Here's how she suggests you can become your strongest:

Start with free weights. It's my opinion that a teenager should start off with free weights when they get involved with any type of strength sport or weight training. This not only helps to develop physical strength and physique, but it also helps to build agility. Weight training helps you develop physically and it also helps strengthen your mind in an incredible way.

Participate in some kind of physical activity. If you're already playing a sport, you are set. But some teens aren't that into sports. Keep up your health and maintain your overall conditioning; you should at least participate in gym class or some sort of recreational sports regularly. Walking, jogging, biking, or swimming are all great ways to develop good physical conditioning. In most cases, you can have fun and get physically fit at the same time.

Watch your diet. Your diet contributes to your strength. If you don't have a good diet, then your body's nutritional needs will not be met. Without proper nutrition, it is difficult to build up the muscles.

Don't worry about stereotypes. Don't be afraid to participate in any sport you like. Don't hold back from your natural abilities because of any stereotype. If you want to lift, lift. I know many teen girls who participate in weight training and even power-lifting competitions.

Don't use performance enhancement drugs. I have seen even young girls who use performance enhancement drugs. I'm a Lifetime Drug-Free World Champion Powerlifter and have succeeded in winning competitions and setting state, regional, national, and world records *without* the use of performance enhancement drugs. An individual can accomplish whatever she sets her mind to just by putting in the hard work and being determined. There may

Pushing Your Limits

No matter who you are and at what level you are doing things, you'll sometimes have doubts that you are not good enough, tough enough, or putting time into the right things. But overall, you're tougher than you imagine. The only way to find your breaking point is to not stop before you find it. It's hard, because sometimes you will fail and not achieve your goal, or you might go out there and look stupid. But pushing yourself is the only way to find your breaking point. And if you keep pushing that point, your breaking point will make you go farther and farther.

—Lauren Jensen is a professional triathlete.

be other girls who are using performance enhancement drugs who seem like they are so strong and they are on top of the world. Don't be influenced by that.

Just remember that everything comes in time. You have to be patient with yourself. Any shortcut that you take now will catch up with you sooner than you think.

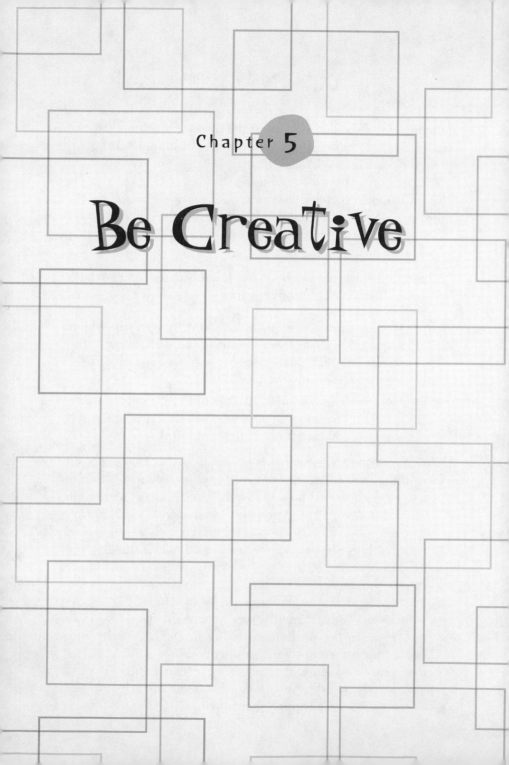

Chapter **5**

Be Creative

❖ Get a New Hobby ❖

Dancing! Reading! Playing lacrosse! Playing the clarinet! Horseback riding! Snowboarding! Designing clothes! Running! Acting! Writing poetry! Rock climbing! Weightlifting!

What's on *your* list of hobbies?

Jill Bauer hosts her own show, *You're Home with Jill,* on QVC, a television shopping channel. The show features everything from what you need to prepare a recipe to decorating ideas, craft projects, and gardening tips. Jill says:

Hobbies have always been very important to me. What's great about having a hobby is that it serves two purposes:

1. Hobbies help you enjoy being alone by yourself. When I was a girl, if I had no one to hang out with, I could still have a good time baking cookies, hitting a softball, or making something crafty.

2. Hobbies help you meet other people with similar interests. Hobbies bring people who have a shared interest together and give them a common bond.

Hobbies have served me well as an adult. They instilled confidence in me and a sense of accomplishment. They've helped me learn to be comfortable being alone by myself. The hobbies you enjoy now are likely things you'll always enjoy. And it will surprise you that in your choice of career, your hobbies often show up. I'm an example of that. I'm the host and creator of a TV show that focuses on many of my favorite hobbies.

My show features cooking. I've always loved to cook. As soon as the prepackaged mixes on my EZ Bake Oven ran out, I was in the kitchen inventing new mixes with flour, peanut butter, and other ingredients. Some worked better than others. My show also features gardening and crafting. I also loved to shop. And look what I do for a living—sell things on TV for a shopping channel!

Some people know right away what their favorite hobby is. They're the field hockey players who live for the game, the dancers who are always at the studio. But others of us aren't so sure. Or we want to branch out and try a new hobby.

Where do you start? Here's Jill's advice about choosing a new hobby. Ask yourself these questions first:

What have you always loved? Did you always want to be outdoors? In the kitchen? Around animals? Building things? Even things that seem silly, like playing with play dough can be clues. That interest might translate into a pottery class. If you liked riding your bikes when you were little, you might want to try racing them. If you like to kick your brother, maybe kickboxing will be your thing. If you just love being around people, you might want to look into volunteer work.

Whose skills do you admire? Maybe you admire a classmate who is an excellent cartoonist. Or you admire a famous actress. These are clues to interests of yours. Why not just give it a try? You don't have to be any good at a hobby; it can be just for fun.

Explore all your options. Some hobbies are obvious, but others aren't. Think about something that has caught your attention. You were flipping through the channels and saw someone fencing, or snowboarding, or building a robot. And you didn't flip the channel for a few minutes. Could that be something you'd like to try?

> **Start a book club.**
> —January, 17, Wisconsin

And a hobby doesn't necessarily have to be something you do. It could be a thing. Say you are the girl who always wears the coolest rings—aha, you love jewelry. Take a jewelry-making class. Say you like lip gloss. Do those craft kits to make lip gloss, or make your own soaps or glitter candles.

Okay, you've picked a potential hobby. Now Jill will help you get started:

Don't feel intimidated. Don't hold yourself up to too high a standard. You think you'd enjoy piano, but get frustrated when you can't play a song after a few lessons. You try golf, and keep missing the ball. Don't give up. Everyone starts somewhere. If you feel intimidated, take a beginner class. Don't compare yourself to others. Everyone learns and improves at a different rate. Hobbies are not a competition; they are to be enjoyed.

Choose your own hobby. Sometimes it is easy to join a club or try a hobby simply because your friends are doing it. But you may miss out on doing something *you* really enjoy. Trying a hobby that is different from your friends' interests allows you to open yourself up to some new friends—to branch outside your clique, to discover more about yourself.

Don't force yourself. Say you think you'd really love to take up horseback riding. You try it a couple of times, but realize your butt just gets too sore. Or you can't stand the manure aspect. Don't feel like you failed. You can still love horses, even if you don't want to ride them. Maybe your hobby will be watching horse shows, instead of participating. That's fine, too. Say you tried to paint, but found it too frustrating. Translate your love of art into trips to different art museums and galleries, or take art history classes instead.

Take a class. Learn more about the hobby by taking a class. Take a class at school or (so you don't have to deal with grades) outside of school. Community groups often offer classes to people of all ages, sometimes specifically for teens.

If there aren't classes in your area, start your own. Say you love to read mysteries but there aren't any mystery book clubs for teens in your area. Start your own book club. Advertise it in your community newsletter's free meeting column, or hang flyers in the library at school.

Share your hobby with your friends. Your hobbies are a great way to bond, even if your friends don't usually participate in them with you. Say you love the outdoors. Plan a scavenger hunt hike for your friends. Say your hobby is fashion. Have a sleepover where you hold a fashion show of your own creations or where everyone brings their favorite outfit for a theme. If you're crafty, host a do-it-yourself night with a bunch of materials out for people to make their own crafts. If you like movies, invite friends over for Oscar night.

Use the Internet. The Internet offers many resources for hobbies. Search for your hobby as a key word and you'll find communities for people who share your interest, lessons, and new ideas. You love to cook but can't afford to take cooking classes? Try new recipes on food Web sites online or join a virtual cooking club. The Internet is particularly good if you are introverted about jumping into something new. You don't have to be as courageous online—you can stay anonymous as you ask your "dumb" questions. It's a good way to get your feet wet.

✤ Make Your Own ✤ Web Site

It seems so weird, but not long ago nobody knew about the Internet. Think of the zillions of Web sites out there for women now. Imagine being the first person to have built the first Web site for women. Aliza Sherman was that person.

Aliza is the original Cybergrrl. She'll help you get started on your own Web site with this advice:

Ever dream of publishing your poetry? Putting those photographs you take or the artwork you do out there for the whole world to see? Ever thought of sharing your diary with others, anonymously?

You can if you have your own Web site!

Every girl should have a Web site of her own. It should be a rule, like every girl should keep a journal and every girl should have her own computer. The best thing about having your own Web site is that you can control what's on it. This is your creative space, your place for self-expression—without teachers or parents or editors or anyone else getting in the way of what you have to say. It is All You, All the Time.

So how do you get a simple Web site online, especially if you don't know the basics of HTML (hypertext markup language), the behind-the-scenes code of Web pages?

Choose a location to build your site. There are several popular Web sites online that actually let you build your own site for free. They make it easy for you, letting you pick things like font size and background color with just the click of a button. If you know how to use a Web browser, then you can build you own Web site. Ask your parent's permission before you go any further. Here are the best sites for building your own site for free:

- **Geocities:** http://geocities.yahoo.com/home
- **Angelfire:** http://angelfire.lycos.com/
- **About.com Personal Web pages:** http://login.about.com/pwp.htm

Register. First you have to register on the site (for free) to get access to their Web site building area. No matter what, you should not have to put a credit card number into a registration form to get access to the Web-building tools.

How do these sites offer this service for free? Well, they put advertising on your site, so you do have to put up with their popup banner ads. But on Geocities.com, for example, you get to choose the type of advertising that appears, like celebrities, travel, or pets.

If you don't want the ads to show up, then you do have to pay a monthly hosting fee. But we're here to talk about freebies!

Use their cool features. These sites have all kinds of tools to make your site rock. You can download free images or upload images off your own computer, design templates, scripts you can copy that put fun features on your site—like quick polls or a guest book that visitors can sign and leave messages for you—or a counter to see how many people have visited your site.

These sites are set up like communities so you can also visit other member sites to get ideas for your site or to make new friends.

Learn HTML—if you want to. Now, if you want to learn more about Web site building and design, lots of online sites offer free tutorials in HTML, such as these two:

- **A Beginners Guide to HTML:** http://archive.ncsa.uiuc.edu/General/Internet/WWW/HTMLPrimerPrintable.html

- **HTML: An Interactive Tutorial for Beginners:** http://www
.davesite.com/webstation/html/

- **Authoring: HTML Basics:** http://hotwired.lycos.com/
webmonkey/teachingtool/

And there are even a ton of sites that give Web site advice
strictly for teens, such as this one:

- http://directory.google.com/Top/Kids_and_Teens/Comput-
ers/Web_Page_Design/

Sure, having a Web site of your own can be educational; but
more importantly, it can be just plain fun!

(If you use this information to put up your own Web site, be
sure to e-mail me and tell me about it at Julia@edevillers.com. I
want to go check it out!)

❀ Embrace Your Creativity ❀

When you're little, you're encouraged to be creative in school. You
sing songs, finger paint away, try out to be the star of the class play.

Suddenly in middle school and high school, creativity falls by
the wayside. You don't hear much about art, music, and other creative subjects. Creative people are sometimes thought of as kind of
weird, artsy-fartsy types. Society doesn't much encourage creativity
when you're over the age of 10.

Shelly Strazis went through that deal. But Shelly's now a freelance photographer whose work has appeared in magazines like
Teen and *Real Simple.* Here's what she says:

I grew up surrounded by people who worked 9 to 5. They
didn't support my dream of being a photographer. They
didn't think being creative would get me anywhere in life—
like my peak would be taking photos at the local mall studio.
But I tried to work at a 9-to-5 job, and I didn't feel like it
was normal for me. And when I decided to give it a try as a
freelance photographer, I discovered I really could make it.

Are you a creative type trapped in a non-creative universe? If so, listen to Shelly's advice:

Expose yourself to the artistic community. Be around people who are creative. See what opportunities are out there. Meet people who share your passion. Absorb the creative culture. Find a support network. The Internet has great Web sites and communities for aspiring artists.

Find a mentor in the arts. Find someone who has succeeded in the area you want to pursue—an artist, a gallery owner, a photographer, a writer. (See page 83 for more on mentors.)

Consider a school or college for the arts. Art school was one of the best experiences I ever had. I lived and breathed photography for four years. I had great teachers who taught me how to love photography even more. But school also taught me to be disciplined and productive with my craft.

Learn the business side of the arts. It's a myth that all artists are poor and starving. But if you want to make a career in the arts, you need to be practical. It is not easy. Know how to make a living and manage the business side of art. You need to know how to handle your money, bill customers, manage your taxes. If you're worried about making enough money to support yourself, learn about jobs that combine business and creativity. Learn to run an art gallery or be an agent representing photographers. Or, plan to have another career and practice your art on the side.

◎ Find a Good Book ◎

Ready to curl up with a good book (after you finish *GirlWise*, of course)?

Karin Snelson was the children's and teen book reviewer for Amazon.com. So she kept up on all the latest and greatest teen reading material. She says:

> When I was a teenager I never read a teen book. I'm not sure if I even knew teen books existed. I didn't discover teen books until decades later when I didn't need them.

Books could have helped. Novels like Jerry Spinelli's *Stargirl* or Susanna Vance's *Sights* or Francesca Lia Block's *The Hanged Man* could have helped me feel more comfortable in my Designated Popularity Zone. It's possible that they could even have helped me resist the pull of peer pressure, that dangerous current that runs through our schools and makes us do stupid things. Books like Robert Cormier's 1974 classic *The Chocolate War* show how horribly far kids can take their desire to fit in. Novels like Laurie Halse Anderson's award-winning *Speak* show that you don't have to (and just plain shouldn't) face your troubles silently and alone. Would those novels have helped put it all in perspective? I think so.

Read.

—Kayley, 13, Washington

We learn from our experiences, but our very identities are shaped by books, too. That's why I wish the right book could magically appear at exactly the right moment in the hands of the teenager who needed it. In the absence of magic, we have teachers, independent booksellers, and school and public librarians who devote their lives to helping teens find books. I never asked a librarian for advice past the age when I couldn't reach the library counter, but I should have. If you go to a search engine like www.google.com and type in "teen books," you'll find Web sites of book recommendations from passionate young adult librarians.

◎ Get Published ◎

Congratulations! Your poem/story/work has been accepted for publication!

Would you be psyched to hear that? To see your name in a magazine, a newspaper, on a Web site, even in a book? Kathy Henderson, the author of *The Young Writer's Guide to Getting Published* (Writer's Digest, 2001, 6th ed.) says this:

Each month, the work of dozens of young writers appears in publications all around the world, whether it's on the Internet or in more traditional forms of publishing.

To do what these people have done, you don't need to be at the top of your class in reading or writing. You don't need to know somebody in the business or have lots of money or years of experience. As many young writers have proven, you don't even need to wait until you are older to try.

So where can you send what you've written?

* Local newspapers
* Letters to the editor columns
* School newspapers
* Magazines, national and local
* Web sites—ones for teens, ones for writers, and ones for special interests, such as hobbies
* Contests
* Book publishers (Getting a book published is the most difficult, though!)

Here's some advice from *The Young Writer's Guide* to help you see your name in print:

Avoid inappropriate submissions. The biggest reason for rejection is something editors call "inappropriate submissions." This means that their particular publication or contest never uses the type of material submitted, say a short story when only nonfiction is used. To avoid making an inappropriate submission, study the market and contest information carefully. Send for and study the guidelines offered. Buy or borrow a sample issue.

Send only your very best work. Rewrite and edit your work until it is the very best you can do. Ask an adult, perhaps a teacher, parent, or a more experienced writer to read your manuscript and offer constructive criticism.

Proofread your manuscript. Correct all grammar, punctuation, and spelling mistakes in your final copy before mailing it out. Make it easy for editors and judges to read your material. When the

Ways to Improve
Your Chances of Getting Published

- Read books like Kathy's *Young Writers Guide;* read the *Writer's Market* and *Writer's Digest* magazines.

- Take classes for writers.

- Join or start a writers' group.

- E-mail an author. Occasionally an author will mentor you or even include your submissions in a book (that's how many of the girls in *GirlWise* got in here!).

- Join chat groups and discussions on the Internet (with parent permission).

- Get an internship in publishing or help out someone in publishing.

- Read, read, read. And write, write, write.

choice is between two works of close or equal merit, the one that looks better will win.

Be prepared for rejection. Most writers have been rejected. Understand that while some manuscripts are rejected for poor writing, others are rejected for reasons not readily apparent to the writer. These include: time needed to print an issue or post it on the Internet, space available for manuscripts, the number of manuscripts already accepted for publication. Rejection is disappointing. It hurts. But rejection must be put in perspective. The editor or judge has not rejected you personally. He or she simply picked another manuscript that better suited his or her needs at that moment—much like you might consider one pair of shoes over another of equal quality.

※ Write a Poem ※

Do you write poetry? Have you thought about trying, but don't know where to start?

And even if the only poetry you read is forced on you in English class, read this anyway, and you might be surprised by a sudden burst of enthusiasm. I was.

College professor Kathy Fagan teaches poetry and is a prize-winning published poet herself. Even her advice to you is poetic:

> I've been reading poems and writing poems since I was a kid, which is a pretty long time; and most of my adult life, which has also been a pretty long time, I've earned my living as a poetry teacher at universities. And the one thing I'm sure of is that there's no right way to read a poem, write a poem, or teach a poem. I don't always understand the poems I read; I can't will myself, as a poet, to write the perfect poem; nor can I explain, fully and without a shadow of a doubt, any given poem to my students in ten words or less. In short, I can't define what poetry is, for myself or anyone else. Just when I think I've got hold of it by the ankle, it wriggles out of my grasp, just as dreams do when we wake up—and that's exactly why I keep reading poetry and writing it and teaching it. I love it because it's alive and naughty and disobedient and willful, surprising and heartbreaking and provocative and frightening—and true, true to itself. The best poems live, as we'd like to, by their own rules.
>
> Having said that I don't know what poetry is but can't seem to live without it, let me say that I have learned *some* things about poetry. There are exactly four things to be precise:
>
> **1. Poetry is everywhere.** Empty your pockets or pack and you've got a poem, or at least material for one. Lint? You can hear a washing machine grinding away, smell the sweet warm heat of the dryer, watch your mother sorting socks, and see T-shirts folded up in a pile like a deck of cards.
>
> Poems are made of this stuff—stuff of the world, the concrete thing-ness of chair, shoe, sycamore tree, sparrow,

manhole cover, tomato. Our world is made of these things, so our poems are, too. Our language is full of the names of these things—words—so our poems have to be. Poetry, therefore, is one way of reading the signs of the world imaginatively. Poems are everywhere if we are in the least bit curious about the world. Almost any poem is found as much as it is written.

Exercise: Write a "found" poem. Try putting together newspaper headlines or personal ads, overheard snippets of conversation, or phrases from a favorite novel or song. Put a little pressure on them and see if they make something like a poem.

2. Most writers of poetry begin by writing it in secret. They are pouring out their thoughts in a diary or journal, making up song lyrics they sing to no one but themselves, writing feverish love poems to someone who doesn't know they're alive, creating imaginary places or people. I began writing that way; every poet I know began that way. We needed to express ourselves, had something to say, thoughts that had to be figured out, feelings that had to be told.

The word "poet" comes from a Greek word meaning "maker." To write poetry is to make, to create. We make images in poems, pictures, stories, songs; we make characters and music in poems; we expose a thing or an object, see it as it is *and* as it's never been seen before. Poetry makes us notice what we've missed. It allows us to understand something we never understood before. It allows us to imagine and speculate, destroy or remember or keep forever. It's different, in that way, from what we tell our friends at lunch or what we write to our grandparents on e-mail or what we write, even, in our essays in English class—because that's *telling* and poetry *shows*. It requires of its readers and writers a unique looking, a unique heightening of all the senses—the powers of observation and the powers of imagination meet up and make a poem. Poetry helps us to use our five senses the way children do to make something new, it makes an abstract feeling or idea into something concrete, something that can be shown to us in words.

Exercise: *Write a poem using each of the five senses: sight, hearing, touch, taste, and smell. Write three short images, one line apiece, for each sense. If you like, number each stanza 1, 2, 3, 4, 5. You'll end up with a 15-line poem full of your own sensuous world.*

3. Anything and everything is appropriate subject matter for it. We know that poetry is everywhere; we know that it should be concrete. That must mean we can write about anything. There's no such thing anymore as "poetic" subject matter because *everything's* poetic subject matter, not just hearts and flowers and heroes. It's all right for a poem to be funny or cruel, ugly or autobiographical, dark or whimsical, rhymed or unrhymed—as long as it's attentive to its subject. The small details are important in poetry, the smallest words—because those details, those words, are important to us, in life.

Exercise: *Write a love poem that doesn't use the word love or any other term of endearment. In other words, don't say, "I love you." Don't tell us how you feel; show us, with all your senses, in word pictures and love rhythms.*

4. Poetry has a mind of its own and lives by its own rules. Make it, give it everything, let it go. How often anymore are you given the chance to play, go wild, lose control? That's okay when making poems. Let your mind wander; be spontaneous, the wackier the better. Don't try to impose any artificial limitations on it—not at first anyway. It's not up to you to make it say something. Let the poem ride on its own steam; it'll say what it wants. Forget your earnestness and best intentions. The poem tells its own truth—isn't that a relief? Let it shock you. Let it sing and swagger. Watch the way the words bump and grind; hear the sounds they make—the meaning is there—in the music, the pictures, the way it leaves you feeling after. Whether it's your poem or the poem of an old master, if it's real, and if you bring your whole attention to it, it'll move you. Just let it.

Read poetry: *Whether your taste runs to Shakespeare or slam, Sylvia Plath, or Saul Williams, read—then read some more, and*

A few good Web sites that accept poetry submissions from teens are:

- CyberTeens.com
- FrodosNotebook.com
- TeenPoetry.org
- TeenInk.com
- TeenWriters.net
- TeenLit.com

read it all. If you hope to write poetry, you've got to read other poets. Even imitate them for a while to learn their tricks. You'll always sound like you. You're an original, and always will be.

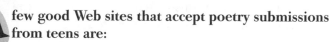

◇ Audition ◇

In ninth grade I auditioned for a school play. And got the lead! I was psyched! (Except it turned out the lead character was named Binky, and I had to wear this really goofy dress with plaid knee socks. And get stuck being called Binky the rest of my high school life.)

Anyway . . .

Auditioning can mean trying out for a school play (hopefully for a better part than a Binky), community theater, a local commercial. Or, hey, maybe you take it a step further and try out for a national television show. Whatever it's for, auditioning isn't easy. It can be totally nerve-wracking. You might feel a lot of pressure, especially if you really want the role.

Harriet Greenspan has been a casting director for more than 20 years as well as a producer. The casting director is the person who watches the auditions and recommends who should get the part. She's worked for ABC and is now doing casting for some pilots for Nickelodeon. She's seen tons of teen actors walk in the door. And out. She's got some advice for you on your auditions:

Try to get information about the role in advance. Get your hands on a script if possible. If you cannot memorize it, try your best to know it well. Sometimes you will be able to get the script a day before and sometimes the same day. You might not have a lot of time to look it over. Just do the best you can.

Get extra help if possible. Ask for help from an experienced actor or an acting coach to practice your lines. Always accept feedback to help you improve. If you don't know anyone to help you and you have the time, call an acting school. See if you can hire a coach or an acting student with experience to help you.

Be prepared. If you're not prepared for a professional audition, don't go to the audition at all. Casting directors have good memories, and you don't want a reputation of being unprepared. Don't take on more than you can.

It's audition time! Harriet has some tips for what you should do to make the most of the opportunity you've got:

- **Don't feel intimidated.** Try to be as relaxed and comfortable as you can be. But also know that casting directors often don't have much time; and if you see a crowded reception area, you can be assured they have a lot of auditions that day. Their patience is limited.

- **Smile and shake hands with everyone.** Say, "It's nice to meet you." Looking people in the eye always helps.

- **Don't ask too many questions.** If it's an audition with a casting director, you can ask her one or two questions.

- **Don't ask: Should I do it again?** If they want you to do it again, they'll tell you.

- **Don't worry if you make a mistake.** Just ask to start again. If you screw up a line or two, don't worry, everyone does it; just stay in character and go on. You might be asked to say the lines a different way. Don't take this as meaning that you are doing

Y ou live in Des Moines, Austin, Cleveland . . . not New York, not L.A. Do you have a chance at breaking into the entertainment business?

Sure! Harriet's tips for you include:

1. Take local acting classes. If you want to be an entertainer, you need to focus on your craft. Your acting teachers may know of opportunities for you to audition for the media.

2. Take other classes that teach you physical skills, such as tae kwon do, soccer, dance. So much of acting is physicality and expression.

3. Highlight any unique abilities you have. Sometimes I am in need of a martial artist, a surfer, a horseback rider. If I see it on a résumé, that person will be a step ahead.

4. Find the biggest city nearby and get an appointment with an agent there. Have your parents check whether the agent is legitimate.

5. You can always make a video of your audition and send it to a casting director in Los Angeles or New York. I get them all the time when I am looking for talent. If we're interested in you, we don't care where you live.

poorly; it is the opposite. It often means they are interested in you and want to see how you take directions.

- **Be prepared to read for someone else.** If you're auditioning for the media, you might get sent next to the producer. This is a good sign. You know you've done a good job when other people want to see you.

- **Say thank you.** When the audition is done, say thank you and leave.

- **When you are done, don't stress over how you did.** Just leave it all behind you.

  If you *don't* get the part, don't be too hard on yourself. But you have to know it doesn't mean you aren't good. It could be anything from hair to height or that they already had someone in mind but weren't sure and wanted to see more people. As long as you went in prepared and did the best job you could, don't try to second-guess yourself.

- **Keep trying.** I have people who are new to the business read for me and they might need more work at first. As they get better, I end up casting them.

☀ Sing Karaoke ☀

You walk into the party and spot it—the karaoke machine.

Uh-oh. You know what's coming.

So does Renee Grant-Williams. She's a singing coach for some, oh, pretty good singers like Faith Hill and the Dixie Chicks. But it doesn't mean she doesn't know how to help the vocally challenged among us. And she's willing to share:

"Hey, why don't you get up and sing one next?" someone yells. Suddenly all eyes turn toward you and someone hands you the microphone. Your mind turns to jelly. Your knees go weak. Sure, you sing along with your favorite songs on the radio, but in front of everyone?

It's only natural to have a pang of anxiety any time you're in the spotlight. But singing with karaoke isn't about giving a perfect performance. It's about having fun with your friends. People want to hear *you*. If they wanted to hear Alicia Keys, they'd buy the CD. Besides, what's the worst thing that can happen? The worst thing that can happen is that you sit there and don't even try. A potential karaoke moment may be lurking anywhere—at a dance, a wedding reception, or a Sweet Sixteen party—so why not be prepared?

Here are some tips straight from Renee that will help make you shine the next time you're in the spotlight:

Pick two or three of your favorite songs to learn. Choose well-known songs that are in your range. Can you reach the high notes without screaming? Can you reach the low notes? Make sure the melody is easy to hum and that you can feel the rhythm easily. Learn the melody and study it as thoroughly as you would study any other subject. Record yourself and listen back. Taking time to write out all the words will help you memorize them quickly.

Try to get the instrumental tracks on cassette or CD so you can sing along without hearing the other singer. If you always practice singing with someone else's voice, you will never learn to lead with your voice. Background tracks to the most popular songs are generally available at record stores and media outlets. Go to the Internet if you can't find them in your town.

Work on your voice. Singing is a very physical activity and requires a power source. Support your voice tone the way you would support your body when you're lifting something heavy. Get your legs under you, tuck your hips under, and use strength from the lower part of your body—as if you were lifting. Push the balls of your feet firmly into the floor. Try not to lift your chin; instead, keep your head rounded over the microphone with your chin lower in the front. This makes the tone sound warm and resonant.

Sing the words. Actually think about what the words mean. It's surprising how much better we sound when we really mean what we're saying. Choose songs that are age-appropriate so you're not trying to be convincing in a song about your six kids and three divorces.

Calm your fears. There's a trick I teach my students when they are nervous about a performance. I tell them to write down all the things they think could go wrong—going off pitch, forgetting the words, falling down—whatever they fear most. Then I tell them to sing and make all those mistakes—just do a terrible job. This is not as easy as it sounds. You'll find it's almost as hard to be terrible as it is to be perfect, but once you've done it a few times, you'll find this exercise helps put your performance fears to rest.

Ham it up. Getting up to sing is a chance to act out your "star" fantasies. Go all the way. Find the "ham" in you. Wear some glam clothing, do some rock and roll moves, sing your heart out. In truth, most people would rather see you succeed than fail, and giving a full-out performance will always go over better than hanging back. Trust me. Things don't improve when you sound as if you're apologizing for giving such a rotten, worthless performance.

Now, I can't guarantee these tips will get you a recording contract or an MTV video, but they should go a long way toward making it a lot more fun—to sing for fun!

❧ Start a Band ❧

Do you go to concerts or watch MTV and think, "I want to be in a band!"

Well, why don't you? Start a band now and, hey, you never know. We could be lining up and sleeping out just to get tickets to watch *you* play someday.

Carla Cherry is a bass player and singer in a band. She says: "Starting a band is not hard as it may seem. Lack of experience didn't stop most groups from forming—why let it stop you?" Here's her advice:

First, decide what instrument you'll play, or if you'll do vocals. If you don't already know how to play an instrument, you'll need to learn. And if you're going to play in a rock band, your instrument will likely be guitar, bass guitar, keyboards, or drums. Regardless of what you choose, you should also try singing, even if it's only to belt out a few ahs and ohs in the background. If you plan to just sing, you should also learn to strum a few chords on the guitar. Trust me. The ability will come in handy later, especially when it's time to write songs.

Get your gear. Musical gear can get a little expensive. It's not just a matter of buying a guitar. You need an amplifier to plug into as well. And once you get together with a group of people who are cranking up a few amps and pounding on a drum kit, you'll also

Music is a powerful force in my life. I've been singing since I was three. I was very shy when I was a child, but if you put me on stage to perform, all of a sudden I became free. And I co-write the songs on my albums, both the lyrics and the music.

You can express your feelings through music. When you listen to my songs, you know exactly what I'm going through because I put it into music. When I get stressed out, writing and listening to music helps me relax.

You can express your individuality through music. For example, my next album is going to be rock instead of pop, which I love because it isn't choreographed. I'll be free onstage to be spontaneous and unpredictable.

—Brooke Allison is a 15-year-old singer
with one album out and another on the way.
She's the vocal artist on the new Disney video, *Cinderella II*.

need a small vocal PA system (plus microphones, stands, and cords) in order to hear the singer(s).

If you happen to know other musicians, you might be able to borrow some equipment, at least temporarily. But if you plan to buy anything, it's best if you can find a knowledgeable friend to guide you. Music stores can be intimidating places even for experienced musicians, and if you go in by yourself, you might end up paying far more than you need to for something you don't really want.

Learn to play. You could take some lessons at a local music store or from a private teacher, or get a friend to show you the ropes. Learning the fundamental chords on a guitar or a few drum patterns will be enough to get you started. Do your homework and keep working on your scales and patterns in between lessons. Covering songs by established acts is a great way to figure out how to put it all together. Your teacher might suggest a few easy rock songs to get started; or if you have some favorites, ask your teacher to show you how to play them. Then practice.

Get your group together. There is no single way to organize a group. Just remember, it's all about having fun. If the people you're playing with are too serious or too casual, and you're not enjoying yourself, then try working with other people. Your first band will probably not be your last.

Maybe you have some friends who want to start a band. All the better! But even if you're on your own, most newspapers and even some music Web sites have classified sections for musicians searching for bands. Find some people with similar musical interests in your area and get together for a trial jam session. For safety reasons, check with your parents before you contact anyone. Bring along a friend the first time you go.

Choose a name. I'm all in favor of choosing a good band name right from the beginning. Having a name gives the group an identity, even while you're still practicing in the basement. Be sure, though, to choose a name that hasn't already been taken. Make a list of possibilities, then check out the names on the Internet and see if they're in use (www.ubl.com, which stands for the "Ultimate Band List" is a good place to start). This will save you a lot of hassle later on if you run into another band with the same name.

Choose your songs. Your group may start out playing some cover songs. Eventually, you or someone else in the band might generate ideas for your own tunes, and you can start building a good set list. Once you have about 30 to 40 minutes of music, and you feel confident enough as a group to hold it together, you can start playing out, because that's what it's all about—sharing your music with people.

Get some gigs. Parties make great first gigs, especially if you're still in your teens and can't get into rock clubs yet. School dances or talent shows are excellent opportunities as well. Let everyone know about your band, especially people on your student council. Eventually you may get a gig through word of mouth. If not, convince one of your friends to throw a party, and off you go.

Write a Song

Y ou don't have to know how to play an instrument to write a song. Think of a past experience or something you feel deeply about. Something that touches you results in a better song. It helps to write the chorus (you know, the part of the song that repeats in-between verses) first because you want to have a hook or a phrase that listeners can remember after the song is over. Once you're done with the chorus, it's easier to figure out the melody. I write the lyrics to the verses last. Like it? Hum the song into a tape recorder so you don't forget it!

—Lexi, a 16-year-old singer-songwriter, recently sang "The Star Spangled Banner" at Dodgers Stadium to a crowd of 50,000 people.

Play. On the day of the show, arrive early and get all your equipment set up well before the audience arrives. You'll also want to run through a few songs to adjust your individual volumes and get comfortable on stage. Also be sure to bring extra extension cords and surge protectors, because you never know where or how many power outlets there will be in the room. Give everyone in the band a copy of the song set list. And before you start playing, make sure your instruments are in tune, that your cords are plugged in properly, and that your volume is turned up.

And now the real fun begins. As soon as you start playing, you'll know what being in a band is all about.

(Hey, don't forget us little people on your way to rock stardom. Be sure to send me some front row tickets to your show, okay? And a backstage pass. And can I get an autograph, please?!?)

Belly Dance

In the privacy of your own room or home . . .

Step 1: Outfit. Put on a pretty bathing-suit top, half-shirt, or bra. Let that belly hang out!

Step 2: Music. Play some music that you love. The best kind for belly dancing has a clear drum beat.

Step 3: Watch Yourself (Or Don't). Get in front of a mirror. (Or find something pretty to look at on the wall.)

Step 4: Assume the Position. Bend your knees. Your feet should be about shoulder-width apart and your knees should be blocking out your toes. Tuck in your booty, raise your chest, and relax your shoulders.

Step 5: Hip Movements. Lift your right hip up toward the ceiling, then let it fall back; do the same thing with your left hip. Think of yourself as a marionette puppet. There are strings attached to the top of your hipbones, and someone is pulling those strings straight up, one at a time.

Step 6: Fancy Hip Movements. See if you can do Step 5 rhythmically with the music. (It is okay if you can't! We're just practicing!)

❀ Appreciate Art ❀

Anybody can appreciate art. That's right, even you. Whether you love to go to museums or are more, "Huh? What's the point?" Whether you consider yourself an artist, or stick figures are more your thing.

Andrea Mulder-Slater is an artist, art educator and art history writer, and the forum leader for Art History on About.com. She says

Step 7: Graceful Arms. Let your arms float up, one at a time, with your elbows rounded. Your palms should be down, and your thumb and middle finger should be a little closer together, like you are holding a tiny plum between them. Let your arms float back down again.

Step 8: Attitude. Repeat Steps 6 and 7 with an enchanting, enticing smile on your mysteriously lovely face.

Step 9: Encouragement. Give yourself some love. Belly dancers like to hiss their approval of each other: "ssss-ssss-ssss." They also call to each other in high-pitched voices, which sound a lot like "Loo-loo-loo-loo-loo!" You can also just yell, "You go, girl!"

Step 10: Nap Time! Take a break. You are a sleepy goddess in a mystical garden of musical delights. This takes a lot of energy so a nap right now would be ideal. (Chocolate is good, too.) Good job!

—Vanessa Carlisle, co-author of
I Was My Mother's Bridesmaid
and a belly dancing instructor.

you don't need to be an expert in order to appreciate art. "All you need are your eyes and some time. The more you look at art, the more you will notice . . . it's really just that simple. Looking at art is no different than listening to music, reading a book, going to a movie, or even eating. The more you involve yourself in any of these activities, the more you will 'pick up.'"

What is art anyway? Andrea puts it this way:

You've probably heard the saying, "One picture is worth more than a thousand words." I think that this old Chinese proverb pretty much hits the nail on the head. Art is a way of telling a story, sharing a point of view, or expressing an idea or feeling. Simply put, art is a form of communication that goes beyond language. Don't believe me? Consider this: You don't need to know how to speak Italian to look at a Leonardo da Vinci painting, nor do you need to understand French to look at an Henri Matisse sculpture.

Abstract art is sometimes difficult to understand. You've probably seen paintings and sculptures that made you say, "What the heck is that?" or "I did that in kindergarten!" Before you walk away from the gallery shaking your head, you have to keep in mind the times in which the art was made. Think about this: Today anyone can fling some paint at a canvas, give it a title, and call it art; but imagine living in a world where no one ever did such a thing and seeing someone do it for the very first time. Throughout history, artists like Claude Monet, Vincent van Gogh, and Jackson Pollock have shocked society by doing something different—for the first time. That's why we know their names today.

One of the main mysteries surrounding the art world is why and how one painting can sell for millions of dollars, while another is worth maybe hundreds. While there are no easy answers, a few truths exist. Generally a work of art is worth as much as what someone will pay for it. Sounds simple, right? Not really. How much a work of art is worth is based on many things, including (but not limited to) these: the artist's reputation, who they trained with, where they were educated, and who owned the work before.

Now you have the background, here is how you can actually check out art yourself.

See art in person. When exploring art, try to view some in a museum or gallery. Nothing you view in a book will ever compare to the real thing. It's not unlike talking to someone on the telephone versus face to face. I can remember the first time I saw a van Gogh portrait "in the flesh." The colors and the brush strokes were so much more vivid than I ever could have imagined them to be. There's a very good reason museums have guards on duty!

Understand and share your feelings about art. Look at a few paintings you like and some you don't, and literally talk about what you see. There are no wrong answers here, so feel free to say anything. Talk about your feelings with friends or family; compare notes.

Discuss the colors and ask yourself why the artist might have chosen the colors he or she did. Do they make sense? Are they hot colors (red, yellow, orange) or cold colors (blue, green, violet)?

Have a look at how the paint was applied and try to determine whether a brush was used, or maybe a palette knife, or perhaps even fingers. The texture of the paint will help you to determine this.

Talk about the kinds of lines you see. Are they straight or wavy? What shapes do you see?

Look closely at the work and see if you are particularly drawn to any other areas. Talk about why that is.

Ask yourself if the painting makes you think of things in motion. Think about how or if the artist is trying to show movement . . . is this achieved with lines or color?

> There will always be somebody who doesn't like you. Don't try to please everybody.
> —Shana, 14, New York

Does the painting look flat, or do you feel as though you could "walk right in"? Discuss where you think the artist might have been standing when he or she created the painting. This can give you some clues as to why the work might have been created.

How do you feel when you look at the painting? Talk about it. (Remember, there are no wrong answers!) Ask yourself why the artist might have chosen the subject he or she painted. Talk about how the artist might have felt about the subject matter.

Don't feel intimidated when looking at or talking about art. Never be afraid to share how you feel, because your opinion is a valuable one.

Express negative as well as positive feelings toward art. It's okay to say, "I really don't like this work." Once you realize there are no wrong answers when talking about art, the freer you will

What to Say
When You Don't Know What to Say

Let's say you find yourself at an art gallery or museum and someone asks you to comment on a work of art. What do you do? You could panic, or stand quietly and sweat. Or you could sound like you actually know what you're talking about by saying one of the following phrases:

"I don't know why, but I am really drawn to this painting."

"The artist's use of color is divine."

"Such a bold statement."

"That's very painterly."

"What a wonderful use of _____ (fill in the blank: color, texture, etc.)."

"Nice balance."

"Very unique and original."

"I love the rough, sweeping lines."

"I like the texture."

"The thick layers of color are very striking."

"The brushwork is very expressive."

"I enjoy the use of perspective."

"The composition is very strong."

"This image is one of mystery and depth."

"I feel the artist's pain."

"That's extremely interesting."

—Andrea Mulder-Slater

feel. When standing and staring at a work of art, accept the fact that your gut can tell you a lot about what you are looking at. If a painting, drawing, or sculpture makes you feel angry, frightened, or sad, try to figure out why. Just because a painting shows up in every art history book doesn't mean you have to love it. Think in terms of food: Some of us like mushrooms and some of us don't.

Chapter 6

Be Caring

❖ Be a True Friend ❖

For my book *Teen girlfriends,* I interviewed more than 150 of you guys to find out about friendships that work. I wrote up a list of what girls said a "true girlfriend" was.

And you know what, this list also applies to guy friends *and* boyfriends, too. So read through the list and put the name of your friends and crushes and boyfriends in place of the "he's" and "she's." Take a look and see how that relationship is going. If your friend doesn't stack up, well, now's the time to reevaluate that friendship to see if it's even worth it. Here are the characteristics of a true friend:

A true friend is trustworthy. A friend is someone you trust who can trust you, too. Secrets are safe with a true friend.

A true friend is there when you need her. A true friend sticks by you in tough times as well as the fun times. You can count on her.

A true friend is loyal. No backstabbing, no talking behind your back. She doesn't act one way with you when she's around other people and differently to your face.

A true friend respects you. He thinks your opinion is important. He doesn't try to push you to do things you don't want to do.

A true friend pushes you to higher limits. He encourages you to do your best. He helps you pursue your dreams. He's genuinely happy when you succeed.

> **Have someone to talk to.**
> —Cecily, 14, California

A true friend likes you for who you are. You're not putting on an act around her. You can act stupid around her. You can just relax and be yourself and know she likes you even more for it.

A true friend listens. She listens when you really need to talk. She doesn't just pretend to be interested. She wants to hear what is really going on with you and how you really feel.

A true friend gives as much as he takes. There's a back and forth friendship going on; it's not just a one-way street. Good friends give you their shoulder to cry on, but then you give them yours back.

A true friend laughs with you. She gets the joke. You act goofy with her, you have fun with her, things seem lighter when she's around.

A true friend is safe. "Friends give us a sense of belonging," said 15-year-old Melissa. "We all have that moment where we walk into a party and feel like we don't know anyone. Or we walk into the cafeteria on the first day of school and wonder where to sit. Then, we see a friend and a rush of relief washes over us. We know where to go."

❧ Stop a Gossip ❧

"You're not going to believe what I heard!"

Juicy gossip.

I know, you're dying to hear it. It's so irresistible to just listen and find out the scoop. To bond with the gossiper because the two of you share a secret. It so much fun—at the time.

But you know what? Gossip is really just a way to bring others down. And in the end, it might bring you down, too. Don't you hate when people gossip about you? You *know* you do.

So when, say, Nikole starts gossiping to you about Jenna, take the high ground. Even if you're dying to hear it. Even if you want to be better friends with Nikole. Even if you're thinking you won't tell anyone. So what can it hurt?

> **Say you're sorry if you screwed up.**
> —Kelly, 15, South Carolina

Gossiping seems fun at the time. I mean *everybody* does it. But think about how often it blows up in your face. First of all, you just know that sooner or later Jenna is going to find out you guys were talking about her. And she's going to feel hurt and angry. And then there's Nikole. If Nikole's so ready to gossip about Jen, then you know what? Next time, it's gonna be you.

Stop the gossiper with these one-liners based on advice from Dianna Booher, author of a ton of books, including *The Worth of a Woman's Words: The Power of What We Say to Build or Destroy, Heal or Hurt, Inspire or Discourage:*

> *"You know, I don't pay much attention to gossip anymore, things get so twisted in this school I don't know what's what. Don't you think?"*
>
> *"I'm surprised to hear you say that. Jenna always says really nice things about you."*
>
> *"Huh? I've never known you to spread rumors that you haven't checked out."*
>
> *"Really? We've got to tell Jenna that people are saying that about her so she can set the record straight. Let's call her now!"*

(So stop the gossip. I totally know, it's reeeeeally hard to do. But give it a try. And then you don't have to worry about the consequences—like losing a friend, like making people feel bad, like pissing people off.

And you know what? Once people realize you're not a gossip, people are less likely to gossip about you.

Now you have to admit, *that* sounds good, doesn't it?)

❧ Respond to Put-Downs ❧

There are always people around who get a thrill from putting other people down. You know who they are. It's sad that the only way they can make themselves look better is by making fun of someone else. But the reality is that lots of people do it. Face it. Some people think it's funny to put other people down and make them feel terrible. But when you're on the receiving end, it's not so funny, is it?

Susan Bishop is the president and CEO of Bishop Partners. She has some ways you can respond when someone is trying to put you down that can help get them to stop *and* make you feel a lot better.

Here goes. You're being dissed. Your first thought is to get upset, to cry, to get mad and fight. But control it and . . .

Don't react emotionally. The person is trying to get a rise out of you. Don't give her what she wants. Don't let her know she's getting to you. If you don't react, then they are more likely to move to someone else. Even if you feel hurt on the inside, don't show it on the outside. That's not being phony; it's protecting yourself.

Ignore it. This is a hard one to do. If everyone is making fun of you, you can pretend they aren't and just go on with your life. If you can do this, more power to you. But if this one doesn't work for you, move on.

Acknowledge it. Okay, suppose what they're saying is true. Consider just admitting it. Someone puts you down because you don't have a date for prom. Be casual about it. Even smile, act like "So what? It's no big deal." Just shrug and say, "Yup, I'm dateless for this one." I remember my friend in high school was giving a report in class and she was really nervous and just blanked out. Some girls, being mean, giggled and were making fun of her. She turned beet red and I felt so bad for her. Then suddenly she said, "I'm just too afraid to be up here in front of you guys. What should I do?" And she made us all feel like we were on her side. Suddenly we all turned to the teacher and backed her up saying, "Give her a break. Don't make her give her speech."

Have a line ready to respond. The person is trying to find someone who won't fight back. Give it right back to them so they know you stand up for yourself. You might say, "Can't win them all," or, "And your point is?" Use humor. A funny comeback often is the best way to turn yourself from the person they're laughing *at* into the person they're laughing *with*.

Laugh about it. Laugh off what the person is saying. Even if it's not funny, sometimes this can make the person go away. But if you aren't truly comfortable laughing about the situation, then don't do it. The person putting you down will know you're just doing it to try to go along with them. And they might keep digging in.

Prepare ahead of time. Once you're there facing someone who's putting you down, it's hard to react in an effective way. But if

You've heard this before, but I'm going to tell you again. Some situations are too much for a person to handle. If someone's in your face all the time, it's time to get some help—from your parents, a guidance counselor, a teacher, a mentor. Let this person know what's going on. Yeah, you might feel embarrassed going for help, but things get so out of hand these days, why not just get it taken care of and then you can move on with your life!

you practice and gear up for the time it will happen (and it'll happen, sooner or later), then you've got a better chance of reacting the way you want to, not the way they want you to. Get a trusted friend, or even your mom or dad, to pretend they're the person putting you down. They might say, "Nice pimple, Zit Queen." And you have to act out what you would do to respond. Keep pretending over and over again. By the tenth time or so, you'll get past it. Role-play until you can respond without getting all emotional.

❀ Get Along with Your Mother ❀

Yeah, that means you.

Melissa Palmer didn't always get along with her mother. She's now in her early 20s and works for Osea, an all natural skin care line that has been featured in most major magazines, including *Vogue, InStyle,* and *Teen People.* Her mother owns the company. Yup, that's right. She works for her mother.

Melissa says, "In a million years I never would have thought I would work with my mother. When I was a teen, if you had told me that, I would never have believed it. I was always a product junkie and I admired her products. But I went off and worked other places. I didn't think I would work for her. And it took some adjustment, but now it works. And we have lots of fun working together."

Here is advice from Melissa, who talked to me, along with her mother Jenefer, about how to get along better:

Appreciate your differences. Realize you're different people with different interests and personalities. My mom's the creative free-spirited type, and I'm a detail-oriented numbers person. We have to work with our differences. But it's great because we play off our strengths, and the other person is there to help cover our weakness.

Show her some respect. I try to keep my feelings in check. I used to take my moodiness out on my mother. Now I try to take her feelings into consideration, too. And I think of her as a person, not just a mom. It's an evolution in our relationship.

> When fighting with Mom, always finish the fight with an "I love you."
> —Harmony, 17, Pennsylvania

Do things together. My mom and I always made time to do things together. We liked to shop, to take walks, and to cook together. We also made beauty routines together, which gave us time to pamper and take care of ourselves.

Listen to her. Your mother can teach you so many lessons. For example, my mother taught me that beauty comes from the inside. I learned eventually to listen to her when she said no, because she almost always did have a good reason.

Try not to feel embarrassed by her. It's natural to get embarrassed by your mother. But I learned that nobody else is noticing that, say, your mom is really noisy when she chews even though you are humiliated. I remember my friends thought my mom was cool even when I was thinking she was embarrassing.

Admire her. I admire my mom for what she has done with the business. She also stayed home and was always available for me and for my brother. There's a lack of emphasis on family these days, so I really appreciate that she has always been there for me and still is.

On Becoming Your Mother

Last year, my husband walked by my mother's wedding photograph hanging in the hallway. "That's not your wedding dress," he commented, thinking it was me. All right, my husband is probably a bad example since he is not usually Mr. Observant, but it's true: I'm becoming my mother.

I fought it long and hard, but now I'm a carbon copy of my mother; we even work together. My mother, Jane Yolen, is the author of 250 books with more awards than I care to try to count. She is just generally amazing. I did not, however, always feel this way. I spent my teenage and young adult years rejecting everything she believes in and stands for in order to find my own person. Of course, once I found that person, I realized how similar she is to my mother. Since I had found her (me, that is) on my own, without my mother's help, I am now able to accept, and even be proud of, our similarities.

Some practical advice for walking in your mother's footsteps:

1. Always accept advice. You don't have to take it, but should always accept it. Be a sponge—learn everything you can.

2. Accept comparisons, but find your own style.

3. Fight for your opinion. You will lose most of the time, but that one time you win makes it all worth it.

—Heidi Elisabet Yolen Stemple

◎ Give Good Customer Service ◎

May I help you?

Welcome! We have a sale going on today . . .

Want fries with that?

Customer service. Whether you work at Hollister, Taco Bell, or the fake hair extension kiosk at the mall, how you treat your customers is key. It's great for the customers, of course, to have someone with a great attitude helping them. But it's also great for you. You feel better when you have a good attitude. And you are much more likely to get raises, promotions, and better jobs.

Barkley Hope is the owner of Barkley Hope: Items for a Princess. It's a hip store on hip Melrose in hip L.A. where celebs like Eve, Carmen Electra, and Minnie Driver shop. One reason people say they love to shop at her store is because everyone who works there treats the customers really well.

Here's what she tells everyone who works for her:

Give a customer what she wants. Remember: Customer service means giving the *customer* good *service*. You should go out of your way for your customers. Here's an example: Say a customer wants the shirt in purple, but we don't have it. Rather than searching everywhere to find it in other stores (maybe it's not even made in purple), we might call the designer to ask if he'll make one in purple for our customer. The customer knows you are taking good care of them. If you can't answer a question, find someone who can as soon as possible.

Connect with the customer. Lots of people in the entertainment industry are unapproachable. There is a law in retail that says if customers act as though they want to be left alone, you leave them alone. I disagree. I think most people want to be talked to if you aren't pushy about it. You might offer them a drink. People get in a good mood eating a lollipop, so I offer them one of the ring pops we have in the store. Flatter your customers, being genuine of course. I might tell someone I like her hair or her belt. And I mean it, but it also gives me a way to connect with the customer.

Treat everyone with respect. I am happy to see every customer who walks into my store. It

> Be nice to everyone!! Be the girl who always says hi to anyone and everyone. You'll love the results.
> —Gina, 19, Indiana

doesn't matter to us whether someone is a celebrity or a teen. We treat everyone the same. If someone comes in all ragged and doesn't look like she has money to spend in our store, it doesn't matter to us. Your customers should feel that they are welcome and you are there to help them.

Have a good attitude. Some people I have interviewed think they are above serving others. They act like they are too good to help people shop, sweep the floor, serve customers tea, or do other menial stuff. But it's your job to serve people, to pamper the customers. And I always feel good when I do it. You won't get far if you think you are above other people.

◎ Be a Manager ◎

You've been promoted. Congratulations!

One day you're working the counter, asking customers if they want extra mayo on their sandwich. Or stocking clothes at Limited Too. Or working as a clerk in the bookstore. And then, you get that promotion. You're now assistant manager or have some important title. You're a boss! Other people report to you now.

It's a whole different ballgame. Cait Pomeroy has promoted many teens to assistant manager in the bookstore she owns. And she sees some do better than others— way better. And here is what makes the standouts stand out:

> **If you have a problem, don't just whine about it. Find a solution.**
>
> —Brittany, 16, North Dakota

Be able to deal with peer pressure. Younger managers have the added burden of peer pressure. You might be managing the people that you were on the same "level" with before. But suddenly you are the manager and being the boss of your friends. And there's a very real possibility you will be walking the halls at school with one of your subordinates. That can be pretty intimidating.

Customer Service DON'Ts

- Don't act like a customer is bugging you when she asks a question.

- Don't complain about anything—such as not having a break, that you can't wait until you're off work, that your manager is being a jerk—where the customers can hear you.

- Don't talk on the phone to your BF while working and make the customer wait until you're done.

- If you're having a bad day, don't let the customer know it.

- And don't forget to smile!

These new responsibilities are not a license to settle old scores. It absolutely does not matter to our bookstore who was dating whom, who gossiped about whom, who had a date to the prom and who didn't. Inside the bookstore, we tell both young managers and employees that it all has to be simply left outside. Once you walk in, it's all business.

Don't play favorites. It is easy to fall into the trap of giving friends the better responsibilities and the better shifts, just because they are your friends. For example, one of the areas we allowed our young managers to take over was setting schedules. We had to watch out that favoritism didn't occur. This can cause other employees to resent the manager and can hurt morale.

Understand the chain of command. Always know who you report to, and who reports to you. Then there are no misunderstandings about who has the final say. This is especially important when there is a problem between you and someone who reports to you.

Don't go on a power trip. Enough said.

Treat subordinates with respect. Don't discuss any employee problems with friends or co-workers inappropriately. When you are a manager, you will be privy to some personal information. It might be tempting to gossip about what you know. But don't do it!

Talk to your supervisor about any difficulties you have. It is important to feel you can talk with your boss freely about problems you are encountering without feeling you're failing.

Being a manager is a major step. Today, you're managing the concession stand, the deli counter, the file room. It just might be your first step to CEO.

Chapter 7

Be Conscious

✧ Simplify Your Life ✧

Homework. Soccer practice. Music lessons. Your job. Religious school. Friend time. Shopping time to get the latest stuff. And 5 million other things on your weekly to-do lists.

Is your calendar so packed that you feel like you don't have time to breathe? Are you exhausted? Ready for some down time?

The New York Times called Elaine St. James the "leader of the simplicity movement," and Oprah called her a role model. Elaine has written five best-selling books, including *Simplify Your Life*. She knows that your life can get crazy and so hectic that it's hard to stop. But here's her advice on how to slow down a little bit and make your life simply more relaxing, more satisfying, and less stressful.

Dare to *have* less. You face a lot of peer pressure. You feel like you have to have everything. But ask yourself, do you really need five more CDs? Another dress? Is it worth working a whole evening at your part-time job to get them?

Simplifying doesn't mean you should deny yourself everything or something you really want. It does mean taking a step back and asking yourself: "Will this add meaning to my life? Or is it just one more thing to get in the way of discovering who I really am?" Be conscious of what you are bringing into your life.

Dare to *do* less. There's so much pressure to be involved in everything. You might feel like you have to participate in every sport, in every school play, in every school club you can fit in. You think the clubs will look good on your college application, or you're in them because your friends are. But you're running yourself ragged.

Simplifying means doing less. Be conscious of how you're spending your time. Examine the reasons you're doing something. Ask yourself, "Am I taking on this activity for the right or wrong reason? Because I really want to, or because my best friend is doing it? Or because I feel pressured to?"

Some reasons are legitimate. Sure, you want to be in some extracurriculars; and sure, it will be good for your college application. But the ultimate thing to keep in mind is you can't do it all. You've got the rest of your life ahead of you to explore what you want to do.

Decide what's really important to you and let the rest go.

Dare to be your own person. In the first two items you asked yourself if you're buying something because of pressure from other people, doing something because of other people. If you are, maybe you need to stop. Make sure you're not living your life for someone else. Bring a new level of consciousness to things you do and have.

> **Take a nap.**
> —Riá, 17, Louisiana

When your focus is acquiring the latest and greatest, when your life is packed with things to do, it's hard to figure out what you really want and who you are. Our lives are complicated enough, without adding a lot of extra stuff we don't really want or need.

Find the courage to figure out who you are. Go with what you know is right. Just dare to be yourself.

It's liberating.

✤ Find Your Passion ✤

What's your passion?

I'm not talking about your crush or your BF, not that kind of passion. I am talking about what really sparks you. What you want to do with, well, your life. Some people know exactly what they love to do. You know, like your friend who seemed to have been born pre-med and is never happier than when she is with a test tube. Or the friend who shoots baskets any chance she gets. Or the friend who can't wait to get to her babysitting job and play with the kids. You're holding my passion in your hand and reading it: books! Reading 'em and writing 'em.

When you follow your passion, you are psyched to get up in the morning to do it. You feel like you are living the life you are supposed to be living. You're in the life that is right for *you*.

Carol Adrienne is a bestselling author of books including *The Purpose of Your Life* (William Morrow Company, 1999). She has some questions (adapted with permission from her book series) to get you started finding out the clues that can lead you to discover your passion.

Step 1: Write down several activities you *love* to do. Say you had a choice of what you could spend your day doing. What kinds of things would you choose?

Step 2: Finish this sentence: "When I was a little kid, I always loved to . . ." When you are little, you don't worry as much what others think. You don't worry about what you are "supposed to like." You just like it. Name some activities that made you feel this way. Do you miss doing them? Do these activities still excite you? These are clues to your passion.

Step 3: Finish this sentence: "I shine at . . ." What are you really good at? What do people compliment you on when you do it? Don't be modest! Look for things that are really easy for you to do. Think of things you may not have been trained in, but are just "good at." For example, you might be naturally good at dancing, writing, talking, teaching, sewing, daydreaming, listening, surfing, or repairing things.

Sometimes we don't appreciate things that seem effortless to us. How about that math homework that's so easy for you even though everyone else is complaining about it? Or how you always help your little sister's friends with their problems? You need to appreciate that you may be a natural mathematician, a natural mentor, a "natural" something. If you enjoy doing it, you may have clues to your passion.

Step 4: Pay attention to your thoughts, daydreams, and interests. Write down everything that interests you for a week. Review what you come up with and watch for any patterns.

Step 5: Finish the sentence: "I am most myself when . . ." Think of some times when you felt like you were truly and deep down the real you. There's a clue.

Step 6: Review your high points. What activities or situations in the past really excited you? Are they still important to you?

Misery loves company; bad company loves other bad company. People who are doing things that are wrong—even though down deep they know they are wrong—don't want people around who aren't doing the same thing, or who think they are wrong for doing it. Sometimes a strong young lady will have to walk alone, and that makes a strong statement. When you get older, your good decisions will prove to be worthwhile.

—Lisa Miree, Miss Black USA 2001

Of all the things you are involved in now, what one or two things stand out as most important to you?

Step 7: Describe someone you admire. This list will be a description of things you would like to do, too. Watch your tendency to think, "Oh, that person has special talents. I can't do that." Ask yourself what you could do to explore or develop these characteristics.

Step 8: What do you keep being drawn to? Now, put together all of the clues. What are common themes? What got you excited when you thought about it? Stay excited . . . and follow your passion.

⊛ Journal ⊛

Are you the journaling type? The kind of chick who has 6 bazillion diaries in your dresser drawer marked "Private! Keep out! This means you!" I was, and I still have those diaries in a box in my basement. (And no, you can't read them, and I will never tell where the keys are hidden.) If you're like that, you're already psyched up to read this section.

But maybe you are not a natural writer type. You hesitate to write because, let's face it—you don't think you're a good writer. Or you don't like writing those papers for English class, which means you won't enjoy journaling, right?

Nyah. I like what Catherine Dee told me about why you might like to journal. She's the author of several books for teen girls, like *The Girls' Guide to Life* and *The Girls' Book of Friendship*. So she knows these things. Here's what she says:

> The experts say journaling is good for you because it helps you get perspective and discover more about who you are. But my favorite reason for journaling is simply that it cleans all the cobwebs out of my brain, the way going for a long walk does. Once you pour your worries, obsessions, fears, and insecurities out on paper, what's left? Just the good stuff. It's not that all my problems vanish, but I feel lighter and less neurotic. It is one of those wonderful free things in life: writing your worries away and then closing the journal and sticking it in a drawer.
>
> I am now the owner of a big box of old journals. I can look back at them any time I want, though when I do, it can be kind of depressing because I'm reading all the bad stuff I got out of my system when I detoxed. At one point I considered burning them to make sure no one would ever browse them, but then I figured that was dumb because *I* might want to browse them.

Let's get started. This is what Catherine says:

Get a journal. You can use anything you want to. A plain old drugstore notebook is what I use. Could even be index cards, computer files, tape recorder. Maybe you'd like a journal with black pages and use florescent pens. Make a journal. You can have links that go to different entries, and links to expand on particular things you're writing about.

Instead of writing a journal, draw it. Or do both. Or decorate the cover of each journal. I used to make little things out of clay like rainbows and ice cream cones and stick them to my journal.

Find time to journal. You might be a creature of habit. Maybe you like to write before you go to bed. Maybe you like to carry around your journal with you wherever you want to—in school, in the car . . . anywhere.

But really, any time you feel burdened with some thought or feeling is a good time to journal.

Start writing. However, whatever you want to. There is no right way to write! Write the date. Then write whatever is on your mind without judging it. Skip around from topic to topic, spew emotions in capital letters, write incomplete sentences, doodle, make lists of favorite things, discuss the same thing over and over. Write poems, imaginary dialogs between you and your crush, and affirmations. Use colored pens or invisible ink. One artist and writer, SARK, writes in different colored pens. She makes lists, writes in circles, and makes art out of her writing.

Celebrate who you are and the great time you've had. Cry with yourself. Plot your next move in life. Let all of it spill into the safe, protected space of your journal—truly one of the best friends you'll ever have.

◎ Write Affirmations ◎

Ever try to psych yourself up by thinking, "I'm going to walk in and ace that test!"

Even if you didn't know it, you're using a really powerful tool called an affirmation.

"An affirmation is a statement of purpose," says Dr. Tian Dayton, the author of *It's My Life! A Workout for Your Mind* and ten other books. It's a way of talking to yourself in positive and encouraging ways. It can be taking something that's tough and turning it into a positive statement.

For example, if you find it hard to speak in front of the class, instead of walking around telling yourself, "I'm so nervous, I can't do it," you turn it around: "I will communicate and share myself and my thoughts in class today." If you're shy, instead of thinking, "Nobody's going to like me," turn it around and say, "I will attract friends with whom I'll have an authentic relationship."

But most of us spend more time on the opposite, putting ourselves down: "I can't do it." "I'm going to make a fool of myself." "I can't be seen in public looking like this." It's more natural to put yourself down. So that's why it's important to make an effort to use affirmations—and because they can make a really powerful difference in your life.

Affirmations are cathartic; they let you get your feelings out. They're a daily way of building your self-esteem. When you affirm yourself, you can be happier and enjoy life more. Affirmations also give you a chance to kick yourself in the butt. But it's a gentle kick—more of a self-caring loving push. Affirmations can help you get through tough situations one day at a time.

> **Give yourself a hug—literally. It feels great.**
>
> —Arielle, 17, California

Tian has a way of using affirmations that she has found *works:*

Write affirmations in a journal. Write about a page of affirmations. Write whatever comes to mind. And then finish up with one sentence at the end that you will carry around with you.

Start with "I" or "Today." For example, "I am good enough as I am," or "Today I will allow myself to feel comfortable in my own skin." Write them in the first person.

Take whatever issue you're working on and put it in a positive form. For example, if you're having trouble accepting your body, affirm yourself with "Today I will appreciate and take care of my strong, healthy body God has given me."

Focus on one theme. Give it a title. For example, if you're writing an affirmation to enhance your self-esteem with lots of positive statements, you might call it "Feeling Good About Myself."

Write a page of affirmative journaling. More than a page tends to be overwhelming. For example, "Today I recognize I am in charge of my own life. Though I need to depend on people and reach out for help and guidance, ultimately it is up to me to make something of my life."

Times to Affirm Yourself

- Affirm yourself when you first wake up, before you even get out of bed. For example, say, "I bless this world as I walk into it. The more I can bless this day, the more it will bless me."

- Take a quiet walk by yourself. Each time your foot touches the ground, affirm yourself: "I have my own, unique place in this world."

- Shut your door, relax, even out your breathing. Go into the silence, and affirm yourself: "I rest in my own inner calm."

- Affirm yourself in bed while you're falling asleep at night: "I let go and allow my spirit to be refreshed through the night."

—Dr. Tian Dayton

Finish with one powerful sentence. Summarize with one powerful affirmation that sums up your theme, such as, "I will like the life I have to the best of my ability," or "My life matters."

Carry the final affirmation with you. Memorize it. Write it on sticky notes and put them in your notebooks, your bag. Put it on your mirror and say it to yourself while looking in the mirror.

Try to write at least one affirmation every day, or as often as you can. It's like cleaning your room. When you don't clean it for a while, it's overwhelming. But when you pick up a little each day, you're less overwhelmed, and living in a cleaner environment.

Tian offers an example of affirmations every one of us can use sometimes:

- Why should I be hard on myself?
- Who will benefit from me disliking myself?

- Each day I can find something about myself that makes me feel good.

- I will appreciate the day God gives me, rather than doing my best to find fault with it.

- I will work with the world today; I will let it be my friend.

☺ Eat ☺

Do you worry about being too fat?

Are you always on a diet or thinking you should be on one?

Do you spend more time worrying about food than enjoying it?

Eating. We need food to survive. But you know how it is—all of this focus on being thin. On dieting. On losing weight. If you're not falling for it, one of your friends is.

Geneen Roth is the author of several books, including *When You Eat at the Refrigerator, Pull Up a Chair.* Her books were among the first to link emotional eating with deeply personal issues that go far beyond weight and body image. She's been on *Oprah,* on *Good Morning America,* in major newspapers and magazines, and is a very well-known speaker on this topic. She knows what she is talking about. SO READ THIS!

The teen years are a great time when you're starting to come into your own essence. Your own flavor. Who you are and who you are going to be. But sadly, at this age there's a big emphasis on dieting and losing weight. And this focus diminishes your development of your essence. It means you're just focusing on getting smaller and smaller. And you end up living smaller and smaller lives.

There's a fat and ugly voice in people's heads that really makes them feel terrible about themselves. Most of us follow what that voice says. "Don't brag about yourself. Don't express your feelings. That food is bad for you. You're too fat. You need to go on a diet. Don't eat anything but cottage cheese and chicken without the skin and salad in front of other people." You need to recognize that that voice is not your friend. It's not telling you the truth. When you listen to that voice, you end up feeling worthless. And then you end up eating. It's a vicious cycle.

I've worked with women who are size 2 and feel fat. I've worked with women who are size 14, 16, or 22 and feel fine. Feeling fat is not the same as being fat. What's most important is that you feel good about yourself. It's not that I am opposed to eating healthfully. I'm certainly not encouraging binges and harmful eating habits. But when you take care of yourself, you make the right food choices.

Geneen says:

Don't diet. Unless a medical professional has set up a program for you, don't be dieting. When you diet, it's as if you are telling yourself: "You are not okay the way you are. You have to deprive yourself." When you go on a diet, you are telling yourself you can't trust yourself with food; you are saying you can't trust yourself with your life. Diets *can't* work. They create in you the desire for what you can't have. If you weren't obsessed with the food before you dieted, you are by the time you finish.

And you are setting yourself up for what comes next—the binge.

Eat what your body wants. Not what your mind wants. When you eat what your body wants, you end up with energy, with radiance; you look gorgeous inside and out.

Eat the way you want to feel. Girls often eat for emotional reasons. They eat out of fear, guilt, or shame. Instead of eating for these reasons, start thinking about the right reasons to eat. Eat to reflect that you are taking care of yourself. Eat the way you would

Hint: **If you feel your eating habits are out of control, please seek help from a parent, teacher, counselor, or therapist.**

to be kind to yourself. As if you trust yourself. Eat as if you already are the way you would like to be.

Don't allow anyone to make comments about your body size. Realize that other people's opinions of your body have little to do with your body. They have to do with these people, their preferences, their values. Tell them that's not okay. Consider responding with humor. For example, if someone says, "I can't believe how much you are eating!" you might respond, "Oh you should have seen what I had for breakfast!" Or you can simply say, "That's none of your business, is it?" and let them know they're out of line.

Eat when you're hungry. Stop when you've had enough.

✳ Be Alone ✳

It's Friday night. Your parents are out. Your brother is out. It's just you and the furniture. You are all ALONE.

Are you thinking, "Ack! Have to call a friend, jump online into a chat room, find someone—*anyone*—to hang out with me!"?

Or can you stop for a sec and enjoy the aloneness . . . ?

When you think of being alone, do you think of being lonely? Bunny McCune is the co-author of the book *Girls to Women, Women to Girls*. She's in the middle of writing a book that encourages you to change that thinking and enjoy being alone. This is what she has to say:

Alone. It is a word that stirs up vivid images and deep feelings. In order to better understand its meaning, I spoke with a number of young women about what came to mind when they imagined being alone. Many saw solitude as frightening. They pictured darkness and isolation. There was sadness on their faces as they described scenes of women and girls who were all by themselves. Images of breakups and lost loves; homeless people and teary-eyed girls in unfamiliar places illustrated the discomfort that these teens felt about being alone. Some admitted that they were afraid of being home alone at night. Others feared being attacked or lost in the woods. For many young women, being alone is a scary thing.

Yet, for a few, solitude was centering and delicious. There were those who envisioned peaceful walks in nature, singing, shooting hoops in the driveway, or curling up in their rooms doing homework.

What is it that leads us to fear aloneness or to learn to embrace it as a way we can discover our own true selves? Certainly in our culture, many things pull us away from feeling truly alone. More often than not we grow up in families, we learn in schools, we live in communities, we socialize in groups. We are linked to each other through telephones, televisions, the Internet, chat rooms, surveillance cameras, cell phones, car phones, intercoms, beepers, satellites, video cams. . . . All of this technology has a purpose: It keeps us informed and safe and in touch with each other. But it can also be a huge distraction from our most valuable connection: our connection to ourselves.

Our media and film cultures add fuel to our discomfort with solitude. Horror movies implant real-life images of violence perpetrated upon women and girls who are alone and vulnerable. Magazines are constantly giving advice on how to be attractive, how to "fit in," how to *avoid* being alone. Television is more likely to show the story of "the girl who meets the guy and lives happily ever after" rather than the tale of a single woman who courageously meets challenges in her life. When was the last time you saw an adventure story about a young woman who is strong, happy . . . and alone?

We will all be alone at some point in our lives. It is inevitable. Yet there are few places where we learn to value solitude.

In my conversations with girls about being alone, I spoke with several young women who had participated in outdoor adventure programs. In experiences such as Outward Bound, these young women faced physical challenges. They survived life-threatening weather conditions and the interpersonal storms that occur when you put twelve strangers out in the wilderness together. Yet all of them describe their solo experiences as one of the most enriching and life-changing parts of their journeys. One 18-year-old girl shared, "When I was alone I could hear myself better . . . the real me. It was easier to focus on what I thought and felt, rather than what everybody else thought."

Another young woman described her fear of being alone, yet when she settled into her campsite, she realized that she felt less lonely when she was alone than she had been for the past few days with the group. A presence surrounded her. She wondered whether it was God or simply her own inner voice. The voice reminded her that she was okay. She was capable. She was strong. She was independent. There, in her handmade shelter in the woods, she had everything she needed. She had finally met her "best friend." Her name was Alone.

I once heard that there is an American Indian word for "lonely" that, translated into English, means "I have lost myself." Ironically, it wasn't until these young women were alone that they found themselves. They realized that they were enough. They were powerful young women. Alone = all one. When we consciously choose to be alone we are whole.

There are some simple ways for you to sink into the wisdom of solitude. The first step is to consciously decide that you are going to make time to be alone and to trust what unfolds.

This may be hard at first. There are distractions. Phones ring. Chat rooms beckon. Siblings bang on the door. Friends stop by. Parents want to talk. Sometimes you will have to intentionally separate yourself from these things, choosing to place a higher value on your time alone.

> You have to learn to love yourself before you can love someone else.
> —Eileen, 19, New Jersey

You may fear what will come up when you are quiet and by yourself. Many of us want to avoid how we really feel. It can be scary. But, Alone is very wise. She knows how to pace your feelings. She knows to trust your tears. She knows to listen until you are done exploring your own true story. She may encourage you to write in a journal, to draw, or to take a walk in the woods. She will tell you when it is time to ask for help.

Trust her. Trust yourself.

The most likely place for you to find yourself alone may be in your own home. Is there a place in your house you really love to be alone? Look around your room. Is it a reflection of the real you? Does it feel cozy and safe? Is it a place you want to be? Does it feel good to be alone there? If not, get creative with your space and let it be an invitation for you to be who you really are. This doesn't have to cost money or take a lot of time. It may be as simple as changing the furniture around or hanging pictures that remind you of what is important to you.

You may need to leave your house to feel truly alone. Let yourself explore a park or a safe place nearby where you can walk in the woods. Many people find that they are most at peace when they are in nature. The trees have a way of making you feel seen. The birds call to you. The wind swirls around you. The sun warms you.

Solitude is a clean canvas upon which you can draw your life. It is the place where you can explore what you love, let your self guide you, and be who you really are. So, before you fill up your social calendar for the weekend, call Alone and ask her out.

She may be shy at first, but she's the best date you will ever have. She knows your heart. She is a great listener. She can read your mind and loves you unconditionally.

Invite her speak to you often and her messages will get stronger. When she gains the courage to voice her wisdom, she will guide you to all you have dreamed of, and it will be your own precious life.

✧ Find Time for Joy ✧

Happiness. Joy. Just taking time to enjoy everything good around you. Doesn't that sound great? Doesn't it sound like the way it should be?

Then why do we feel so miserable half the time?

Padi Selwyn is the co-author of *Living Your Life Out Loud: How to Unlock Your Creativity and Unleash Your Joy.* I'm just going to let her tell you about what she knows about joy . . .

> When I started writing a book several years ago, a good friend asked me what it was about. "Joy," I told her.
>
> She seemed surprised. "Joy? I never think about it."
>
> "Well," I replied, "That's why I'm writing about it. Most people never do."
>
> And that's the problem! How can we expect to be happy and joyful if we never think about it, if it isn't really important to us? I believe that in order to be truly happy and filled with joy, we have to think about it. More importantly, we have to do something about it on a regular basis.
>
> Now, I'm not proposing that we can all stay blissed-out every day. That wouldn't be very realistic. Certainly, there are days we feel angry, frustrated, maybe even depressed. But unless we learn how to change our emotional state and tap back into the joy in our lives, we won't be as happy as we could be.

So, how *do* we bring more joy into our lives? Padi says . . .

Realize that you cannot control all the things that happen to us, but you can control how you react to them. It's up to us to control our reactions and emotions to what happens in our lives; that's our responsibility.

Find something that brings you joy, and have it around. As a native New Yorker, I was particularly upset about the devastating events of September 11. I had relatives who worked both in the Wall Street district and at the Pentagon, and it was a terrifying day till we found out that everyone in our family was safe. As were many others, I was shaken for weeks after the event.

One day, I realized that in my grief, I had not put on any music in the house. Normally, I always listen to music; it is a source of great joy to me. So I started playing my favorite CDs again. Just that small act of bringing music into my life again helped me start to feel better and happier.

We all have activities that make us feel better when we're down. Perhaps for you, it's talking to a friend, taking the dog for a walk, listening to music, writing poetry, drawing, or planning a special event to look forward to. Most people spend more time planning Christmas than they do their lives! If you take time each week to plan how you're going to spend your time, you'll always have joyful expectations and experiences.

> **Stop and smell the roses.**
>
> —Monet, 13, Georgia

Make a Joy List. Why not keep a list of what makes you happy? Add to it every day, as you think of new ideas and recall activities you may not have done for a while. They can be as simple as reading fashion magazines with your best friend, or as involved as going on a ski trip. Keep this list where you can see it every day, and when you feel the need to bring more joy into your life, you'll have a customized list of joyful things you can do or plan for. By making a Joy List, you will be taking the first step to making joy a priority in your life. When you make it a priority, you'll make it a reality!

❖ Volunteer ❖

We've got a mother-daughter team here. They wrote a book together, write an advice column for the Girl Scouts Web site together, and now will show you how you can get out and volunteer together. (Well wait, you don't have to volunteer *with* your mom, but at least go out and volunteer.) They are Harriet S. Mosatche, Ph.D., and Elizabeth (Liz) K. Lawner:

Step 1: Find out what's needed in your community.

HARRIET: The first step is a critical one. There's no point doing something when the need doesn't exist. And since every community can use help somewhere, do your volunteering where it will serve a real purpose. How do you gather this information?

Read your local newspapers—they often include information about volunteer opportunities. Talk to your parents and your friends' parents—perhaps they've heard about an agency or organization that could use some help. News stories on radio and television offer other possibilities when you're gathering information. Maybe an animal shelter in town is being overrun with strays after the holidays. Perhaps a new senior citizen facility would welcome young people as volunteers. Those are the kinds of stories that could present you with just the volunteer experience you're looking for.

LIZ: Sometimes ideas for volunteer opportunities just come up. For example, with my Girl Scout troop, I entertained residents at a nursing home on Valentine's Day for four years because my grandfather happened to live there, and I knew that without us they wouldn't be doing anything special on that holiday.

Step 2: Decide what issue you'd like to tackle in your volunteer work.

HARRIET: If you've done your homework, you've learned about a variety of different problems in your community. Choose one on which to take action. If you have a hard time making that decision, ask yourself some questions: Would you like to work with older people, young kids, or animals? What one topic interests you more than any other? (Is it literacy, child care, disabilities, abandoned animals, housing shortage, substance abuse?)

LIZ: I'm really interested in working with little kids, so I volunteered along with some of my friends to teach sports skills to 5- and 6-year-old Daisy Girl Scouts. I also babysit, but I get paid for that most of the time.

Step 3: Decide how much time you have for volunteering.

HARRIET: Are you available one afternoon a week? One hour a day? One weekend a month? To be fair to yourself and the place where you're volunteering, your expectations and theirs should coincide.

LIZ: Once you start your volunteer experience, you should keep a chart of what you've done, and how much time you've spent doing it. That way, when you need the information (maybe for a college or job application), you'll be ready.

Step 4: Find others who are interested.

HARRIET: Step 4 involves getting together to volunteer with a friend or two or three, your family, members of your Girl Scout group, or other youth at your house of worship. If you prefer to volunteer on your own, you can create your own program. But it's often more fun and more productive if you team up with others. Just be sure that the people you plan to work with share your interests. If you're passionate about reaching out to those who are mentally retarded, find others who care in the same way.

LIZ: My 16-year-old brother started a tutoring program at the public library with one of his friends, and they recruited about fifteen other tutors to work with them. That way, every weekday, at least two or three high school students are available to work with younger students. And I've heard that the high school students have fun hanging out at the library together.

Step 5: Volunteer.

HARRIET: By the time you get to step 5, you're ready to actually volunteer. You know how much time you have, when you're available, what kind of work you'd like to do, with whom you're volunteering. Now, spell all that out in a letter or e-mail to the organization (library, homeless shelter, after-school program, and so on). And don't forget to provide your qualifications. If you're failing your English classes, volunteering to tutor language arts at the library would probably not be a good idea. And if you're allergic to cats, volunteering at the pet hospital doesn't work either. You might include a résumé, which summarizes the skills and experience you will bring to your volunteer work. Before sending out your e-mail or letter, ask a parent to review what you've written. It's important to involve an adult in your family anyway, since you'll probably need a parent's permission before you can begin your volunteer work.

LIZ: The book my mom wrote with some help from me, *Girls: What's So Bad About Being Good? How to Have Fun, Survive the Preteen Years, and Remain True to Yourself* (Prima, 2001), contains a sample letter that could be helpful in applying for a volunteer opportunity.

HARRIET: Although it's discouraging if the place where you want to volunteer turns you down—maybe you're too young or you don't have the right kind of experience—don't allow that rejection to turn you away from volunteering. Find out why you were turned down, since that information will help you decide how and where to pursue other volunteer venues. Every community has many opportunities—you just have to find the one that works for you.

LIZ: When I volunteer, I feel really good knowing that I'm helping other people. And usually I have fun, too!

Do Three Simple Yoga Poses

Want to relax, get in better shape, and reduce your stress? Try yoga. Yoga is the hot new thing. Well, not exactly new, I guess. It's been practiced for about 5,000 years.

Sarah Thomas-Fazeli, a yoga instructor, explains why: "Yoga is part of a body–mind system that combines breath, physical exercise, and meditation to bring about the very best you. Yoga's physical poses bring about countless benefits, including physical attributes like strength, tone, and flexibility, as well as mental improvements in focus, control, and calmness."

Test the waters. Try these three simple physical poses that Sarah suggests:

Child's Pose. Child's pose can rejuvenate and relax you. From an all-fours position, press your hips back so they rest on your heels. Stretch your arms out in front of you and rest your forehead on the ground. Breathe smoothly and feel your breath expand in your ribcage, belly, and back. Imagine lots of space in between each vertebra—the air you breathe in lengthening you all the way from the tailbone up through the neck. Imagine the spinal cord goes even further, all the way through the top of your head. Rest here as long as you like. For variation, adjust the arms to lengthen down next to your sides.

Downward Facing Dog. Strange name, but it offers benefits, such as improving concentration and energy levels. Kneel on all fours, keeping your back flat like a table. After a few breaths, adjust the feet so they are pressed sole-to-floor as you straighten your legs and press into both hands. Your body resembles the shape of a jackknife. Engage the thigh muscles (think of squeezing them, or hooking your kneecaps up into your thighs). Press through the arms and keep hips lifting high toward the sky. After a series of five slow breaths, come to sit on heels. Gaze out in front of you toward the horizon.

Full Cobra. Full cobra can help with your digestion and with menstrual cramps. Lie on your stomach with hands under shoulders, palms open, and your toes facing the floor. In smooth succession, lower your nose, chin, then your chest toward the floor. Then use your back muscles to lift the upper body up and away from the floor. Do not overarch the back, which will cause strain. Gaze ahead, head lifting, neck in line with your spine. Keep elbows bent and rotating inward slightly. For a modified floor version, simply rest your elbows (in line with the shoulders) on the floor in front of you, bringing the hands, in loose fists, toward each other.

❀ Give Back to the World ❀

You probably read Jane Yolen's book *The Devil's Arithmetic* in English class. Or maybe your parents read you her Caldecott-award

Meditate

Meditation calms you, relaxes you, and unclutters your mind. Here's a basic meditation to get started.

- Find a quiet, uncluttered place. Sit with a straight back and close your eyes. You can sit cross-legged on a cushion or on the floor itself, or upright in a chair.

- Now, focus on your breath. What sounds easy is actually pretty hard to do at first, but with practice, the mind will wander less. If your mind is noticing everything but your breath, try counting your breaths by starting with "1" on an inhale and counting "2" on the exhale. Continue like this—odd numbers on inhales and even numbers on exhales—until you reach 10. Then begin again with 1. If you find yourself on 12, 20, or even 36, don't worry about it. Just go back to 1.

When starting a meditation practice, be realistic with your goals. For a beginner, trying to meditate for an hour at a time is difficult and will only discourage you. Try two bite-sized meditations a day, such as 15 minutes each, or just one 15-minute meditation in the morning. Gradually work up from there, one breath at a time. This is just one of many ways to meditate. Try others, too!

—Laura Shin is a yoga teacher and freelance writer.

winner *Owl Moon* during your sitting-on-their-lap stage. She has written more than 200 books.

So you can tell, she has a lot of great things to say. And here is what she wanted to tell *you:*

I said this to my daughter when she was growing up—and to my eldest granddaughter who is now 18. I expect to say it to my other granddaughters when they reach their teens.

I hope that you will leave the world a better place than you found it. We humans are all litterbugs, both in the literal sense—throwing out paper trash is the least of it—and the moral sense.

For my own daughter, that has meant writing books, adopting children, teaching adult literacy, helping battered women.

For my granddaughter Lexi, who was once a foster child and then adopted by my daughter and her husband, it has meant bringing gifts to the shelter where she lived for a number of years. It means helping in a battered woman's home. It means bringing canned goods with her grandfather to a place that collects for the local poor. It means giving part of her Christmas money to various charities. Counseling friends. Joining a gay/lesbian support group because of her best friend, David.

There are many ways to make the world a better place. Litter begins at home. So does the cleanup process.

(Inspired, anyone?)

◎ Connect with Girls ◎ from All over the World

You've got friends on your street, in your neighborhood, around town . . . maybe you've kept in touch with some who moved to different states. But do you have any friends in other countries? Expand your horizons. Connect with girls around the world.

Sherry Handel is the CEO and president of Blue Jean Media and author of *Blue Jean: What Young Women Are Thinking, Saying, and Doing* (Blue Jean Media, Inc, 2001). Her Web site, Blue Jean Online, has had more than a million visitors from 95 countries. Sherry says:

> Getting to know girls in other countries can seem intimidating at first. There can be a fear of not having anything in common. You might think, "I don't know anything about Bangladesh, so what do I have to say to someone who lives there?"

But once you connect with girls from around the world, you realize you don't have to know anything about where they live. For one thing, you will learn. And you'll realize all girls share the same feelings: happiness, sadness, excitement, horror—we just have different cultures.

Sherry offers ways to connect:

Hit the Internet. The Internet offers a huge opportunity for girls to connect worldwide. Blue Jean Online is an example of a Web site where girls from all over the world can connect—and safely, too, as safety is always a consideration online. For example, there are many Web sites where girls can sign in and become members. They then get a member name that doesn't identify their real e-mail address. So they can be incognito. These Web sites often have chat rooms, bulletin boards, and instant message opportunities to get to know other members from all over the world.

Write to pen pals. Despite the online opportunities, traditional snail-mail pen pals still thrive. There's still something to be said for opening your mail box and finding a letter from another country, the international postmark, the foreign stamp . . . and reading someone's actual handwriting.

Start a zine/read a zine. A zine is a hand-made, self-produced publication that provides its writers with an outlet for creative self-expression. Though once associated strictly with all things independent and underground, zines are now making their way across the country and around the world. When you start a zine, you can publicize it to girls all over the world who will read what you have said and may respond. Reading zines helps you read voices of other girls. You can get involved on their Web sites or write to the editors and connect that way.

Join an organization. Take up a cause! Help out an organization. There are many organizations that don't care if you are a teen; they are simply grateful for the extra assistance of another person. Think about something you are passionate about, and chances are there is an organization for it. Many organizations bring together girls from all over the world who have a common interest. They also offer opportunities for travel to other countries. Some teen girls serve as representatives for the organization and travel that way, while others offer camps and study programs.

Travel on a student exchange program. Student exchange is done through your school or organization. You spend a period of time staying with a family abroad, and sometimes their teen reciprocates and stays with you. Student exchange is a big commitment for your family, but can provide you with a valuable experience. Check with your guidance counselor to find out what your school offers.

Travel abroad. Some girls have the opportunity to travel abroad with their family and friends without a formal program. Of course, this can be a great way to connect with girls where you visit. Other girls travel through study abroad programs designed for students. These programs are great for your college applications, as colleges love to see international experience. Check with your guidance counselor. There also are great books on how to study abroad, and the Web site offers a wealth of information.

Student travelers often congregate in the same places and meet each other. There can be an instantaneous bonding experience when you are all visitors in a common country.

◎ Enjoy Nature ◎

I have to confess I am totally an indoors person. I'm never the first person to suggest camping, hiking—even a picnic in the woods. I still have nightmares about a summer camp counselor experience I attempted at a sleep-away wilderness camp. I lasted twenty-eight days, finally going home with an average of, oh, one injury per day. I ignited my hair making a campfire. A bug flew in my eye (which doesn't sound so bad until I tell you I had to go to the hospital to get it removed—ewwww). Of course I got poison ivy. I finally had to give up and retreat to my home in the suburbs. But a part of me envies the girls who are out there—whitewater rafting, rock climbing, hanging out and communing with nature.

Melva "Nikki" van Schyndel teaches skills of the naturalist, tracker, herbalist, survivalist, and scout. And after I heard what it was like for her, I found myself genuinely wanting to join her outside.

My favorite place to be is at my secret place. It is here at the edge of a field, alongside a small pond that I can forget the responsibilities and pressures of life. My secret place is my escape, without limitations or expectations, and where there is nothing to prove, to be, to worry. I can be me. Being so close to nature has not only taught me about myself, but helped me to discover my true self and become the person I have always dreamed of, in a time when it is very hard for us to do so.

In our world where we are told to focus our eyes on one thing, where our senses are dulled from overstimulation and pollution, it is no wonder many people's lives seem mundane. We must open our senses in order to truly listen and see the world around us.

It is truly amazing when we notice what has been happening around us, in nature and in our daily lives. Plants and trees are one of the most disrespected and overlooked allies we have. We learn to understand the language of the birds. Birds don't just randomly sing. In fact, each bird has a wide range of voices and calls, specific to particular circumstances. We begin to see the world looking through new eyes and develop a much greater awareness, of ourselves and the world around us.

Fear is the greatest challenge and the greatest teacher for many people in nature. Our cultures are full of fearful myths about nature, and you will discover many of them to be untrue. The reality is that I am more likely to be hurt while driving to my friend's house than I am to be attacked throughout my whole lifetime by the cougars roaming where I walk every day. Perhaps you will like the rain once you actually let it fall on you, even though people often refer only to sunny days as "nice" in our society. Maybe you will even grow accustomed to the beauty of insects all around you. Disliking such natural things is simply fear and separation from nature. Visiting my secret place has replaced fear with wonder.

It is only in nature that we can find answers to all the questions we ask, where we can feel with our hearts what those answers are, without the distractions of life and our city mind. I encourage you to seek out your own secret place, a place for thinking, relaxing, playing, exploring. A place of sharing or being alone. Discover that whole new world of nature anywhere and begin witnessing all the amazing, magical things that will happen there and in your life.

✕ Be Resilient ✕

Everyone has bad days.

Sometimes it can seem like your life is just one bad day after the next. One of the most important lessons to learn in life is how to be resilient. When you are resilient, you can recover from and adjust to changes, including the bad stuff that happens.

Take it from Bonnie St. John. Bonnie has had some really tough times. But she didn't let the tough times ruin her. She shares what she learned to get through the hard times; she became an Olympic ski medalist, a Harvard honors graduate, and a Rhodes Scholar. She went on to become a White House official, founder of her own business and an author of several books, including one called *Succeeding Sane: Making Room for Joy in a Crazy World.* Here is Bonnie's advice:

Don't lose perspective. When things are going wrong, it's easy to feel like it's the end of the world. It's easy to feel like it will be like this forever.

It won't.

Know what lifts you up. Plan ahead by learning about yourself and what it takes to get yourself out of the hole. For example, when I am in a rotten mood, I need to work out. But for other people, that wouldn't help.

I see three different types of people. *Mental*-focused people often feel better by losing themselves in a good book, journaling, or having a good change of environment. *Physical* people might feel better by working out, or trying a new activity. *Spiritual* people often need to talk to a close friend or a religious advisor. Which are you?

Line up your resources ahead of time. Let's face it: We all know we will need to be resilient at some point when tough times happen. So make sure you know yourself and have things in place for when something happens.

Practice making yourself feel better when you don't feel horrible. That way, when you do feel horrible, you will know exactly what you need to do to get out of it.

Recognize that change is a part of life. It's a fact of life that things change, and realizing that they will change will make you more resilient.

Imagine a better future. When life seems horrible, imagine the future and how things will be different. If you feel ugly and nerdy, imagine the day when you are gorgeous and glamorous and happy. If money is tight, dream of being rich, and what it will take to get there. You are affirming that the problem is not permanent!

Change your environment. This can seem difficult to do as a teen—after all, you can't book a flight out of town for a weekend away without a lot of work (getting permission, raising money, finding a chaperone, which you probably don't want anyway!).

Instead, try getting involved in activities outside of your high school. Volunteer in the community. You will see a drastically different environment, and it will help you appreciate what you have and who you are. If everyone put their problems out on the street like trash, you would probably be glad to see your problems compared to everyone else's!

Have several different groups of friends. In my research about how little kids are socialized, I saw that little girls rely on three to four close friends, while little boys rely on three to four *groups* of friends. Having more than one group of friends is vital to resiliency. Make sure you have two, three, or four different groups of friends that don't overlap at all. We're human; and if one group of friends becomes uncomfortable (for example, because their activities are not in line with your values, or because they are not treating you well), then you have other people you can rely on.

Join a group outside of your school. It could be a sports team, arts club, a job, or Girl Scouts. Being active outside of your high school can go a long way in helping you establish different groups of friends. When I was a teenager, I joined a ski racing group outside of school. It was wonderful to have friends of different ages, from different schools, and with different interests.

Stay active. When you are by yourself with nothing to do, your mind can get a hold of you much more easily and keep you down. Go out and *do something.*

❖ Deal with Rejection ❖

You're not invited.

You can't come with us.

I'm breaking up with you.

You're not right for our group.

Buh-bye.

Ouch. Rejection.

Kathy Buckley is a comedian and an actress. If you think about it, there aren't too many jobs that face more potential rejection than comedians and actors. A comedian isn't funny one night? She's heckled and boo'd off the stage. An actor auditions for a part. She's told she isn't good enough, not right for the part, doesn't look good enough, and is shown the way out the door.

> Never seek a permanent solution to a temporary problem.
>
> —Jamie, 17, Minnesota

Well, Kathy has been nominated four times for the American Comedy Award as Best Stand-up Female Comedienne; and she has a one-woman show and her own special on PBS. Doesn't sound like much rejection? Well . . .

Kathy has faced more rejection than most of us. And she doesn't let it bother her. In fact, she has even learned to embrace it:

When I was a kid, I was six feet tall, nearly deaf, with a speech impediment. I wanted to fit in, more than anything. I even stole candy and money from my parents to give to my classmates to buy their friendship.

Before and After— September 11 and Beyond . . .

You imagined the journey of the rest of your life, and it was a fun trip. The people, the places, the faces. Suddenly, your world became different. It's post-September 11, and everything you thought you knew is gone. The world is a different and scarier place.

What happens to your hopes and dreams? What do you do with your fears?

The effects of a tragedy can hit you immediately, six months later, or years later. You might not even realize you're having a reaction to those specific events.

Keep an eye out for these signs in you or your pals: nightmares, inability to concentrate, flashbacks, disturbing images you can't shake, startle reactions, bad reactions to events that remind you of the trauma, insomnia. If you're having one or more of these reactions, and they are interfering with your everyday life, it's a good idea to seek professional help. Try talking to your parents, guidance counselor, a favorite teacher or another adult you relate to, or a member of the clergy. The act of talking can heal by causing positive changes in your brain chemistry. Emotions release chemicals into your body. Good emotions release good chemicals; bad emotions release bad chemicals. Getting rid of the bad feelings is healthful, but it's important to do it in a positive way.

Writing in a journal is a positive way to gain an understanding of your thoughts and feelings, and to give you a better understanding of what you're going through. Trust your inner voice to speak the thoughts you're too afraid to face. You can write them down and never look at them again, or you can write them down to read years from now when you're safe in your future.

—Rebecca "Kiki" Weingarten, a trained psychoanalyst, coordinates youth programs for the City of New York.

It didn't work. They still rejected me.

I realize now what a stupid mistake I made trying to fit in.

Because whenever you have to *try* to fit in, it's a sign you're trying to be with the wrong people. When I was younger, I was constantly being rejected by people I wanted to hang out with. It was really painful. Now I realize that every rejection meant that I was on the wrong path. Being rejected is a message saying: "You're on the wrong path. That was not where you are supposed to be. That is not who you are supposed to be around."

When I was trying to pitch my television special, I faced a lot of rejection. I had to fight the ignorance of people who said, "A deaf comedian? She can't be funny." And watch as the doors slammed in my face. But I realized that those people were a waste of my time anyway. If they rejected me for those reasons, they just didn't get it. They weren't right for me to work with in the first place. And then, when I found the people who said, "Yes! We want you!" I knew that was the place I should be. Don't spend your life trying to meet the expectations of other people. Don't obsess over trying to be accepted by others.

If there's a part of you that still wants to be admired by others, here's the secret to that: Find out what makes you happy and do it. When you're happy, that's when everyone wants to be like you.

And when you are rejected because of the way you are, don't take it personally.

The truth wasn't that I was worthy of rejection. The truth was *they* weren't worthwhile—for me.

✧ Stop Sabotaging Yourself ✧

What does this mean? Basically when you're sabotaging yourself, you are limiting yourself. You're preventing yourself from being the best person you can be, from having the most fun you can have, and from being truly empowered.

I was really fascinated when I talked to Carol Adrienne, best-selling author of books like *Find Your Purpose* and *Change Your Life,* about this topic. Carol says there are common pitfalls of teen life. You're probably dealing with one or more of them right now. But if you become aware of them, they will be less likely to hold you back.

Check these pitfalls out to see if any of them describe you. Don't be too hard on yourself; almost everyone will see themselves in at least a few. And then, read the suggestions on how you can stop sabotaging yourself and get out of your own way.

Do I lack good judgment? Do I jump into friendship or intimacy too fast? When I commit too soon, does it make me feel trapped? Do I ignore my instincts? Do I choose situations that are against what I really value and want to have in my life?

If yes: Stop sabotaging yourself! Give yourself adequate time to make a decision. Always keep in the back of your mind the idea that you are a strong person. You can take your time. You can make up your mind when you are ready. You can disregard the pressure that others put on you and stay true to yourself. Listen to your body. If you have that sensation in the pit of your stomach that something isn't right, don't make a decision until you think it through.

Am I a people pleaser? Do I always try to please everybody by using many different personas? Am I flattering, too flirtatious, too nice, or too ready to give in to what someone else wants? Do I do things just so other people like me? Do I always agree with other people just to keep the peace? Do I always give in?

If yes: Think about how you can have more integrity. To have integrity is to stick to your own values and beliefs. When others are trying to get you to go along with behaviors that don't feel right to you, acting with integrity gives you self-respect.

Do I crave recognition? Do I always want recognition for everything I do? Am I really doing things just so other people will admire me or pay attention to me? Do I try to get in good with a boss or teacher just because she is in a power position? Am I always out to impress?

If yes: It's not bad to want to excel, but when you find yourself doing things just so you can get compliments from others, you are

"Are you an outsider or an insider?"

That's the first question documentary director Stephanie Walter Williams asks people when she interviews them. She goes on to say:

The real achievers are the ones who answer, "I was an outsider, wanting in."

I just finished interviewing thirteen celebrated women. Every single one of them said something like, "I didn't fit in," "I was a loser in high school," or "I was an insider but the people on the outer margins attracted me." Sure, it's exciting to be beautiful and popular in high school. But after high school ends, the really *cool* people are those people who are more than that; they're the ones who haven't really conformed to what others expect them to be. Look around you and you'll see that geeks rule now. It's the truth!

Enjoy being different. Yes, it takes courage. But now I realize how lucky I was to be the outsider. If you feel like you don't fit in, you should be hugging yourself. Not fitting in can only mean that there are bigger plans for you.

doing it for the wrong reasons. Practice doing things that will make you feel proud of yourself, but don't tell anyone else. Do some anonymous nice thing for someone else, and let the good feeling seep into you. Be committed to excellence just for its own sake. It will be a big relief and you will find yourself staying more true to yourself as well.

Do I talk too much? Do I have to control the conversation by always talking? Do I always talk about myself? When I notice people distancing themselves from me, do I talk faster to keep a connection going? Is it hard for me to listen? Do I interrupt serious talks with jokes or silliness?

If yes: Sure, we all talk too much at times. But when it is a habit, you have to ask yourself why. Do you want to be the center of attention because you want others to notice you? Are you uncomfortable with silence? Try catching yourself when you get too talkative. Learn to be comfortable when others are being heard, too.

Am I suspicious or secretive? Do I feel like I have to keep certain ideas to myself so others won't steal them or do it first? Do I feel like I am separate from most people?

If yes: Being suspicious is often a sign that you aren't getting much support from others. It's good to make time for yourself: taking a long walk, reading, thinking. But other times you may be just hiding out from the world, and it is a cry for attention. You need to have a support system of family, friends, and people you care about and trust. Try to figure out why you are not trusting someone. Do they deserve your suspicion? How can you practice being more open with other people? What makes you feel safe? What people make you feel safe?

Do I resist authority? Do I see myself as the lone ranger or a rebel? Do I think I am the only one who sees things the right way? Do I complain but rarely do anything constructive to change it? Do I have a friend who resists authority and feel a thrill when they act up?

If yes: If you tend to feel that most people are jerks, especially older people, you may be angry about something you can't do much about. Feeling angry and feeling powerless to change anything usually make the whole world look pretty bleak. There are a lot of good reasons to feel angry. But the important thing is to get back to being the person you are meant to be—and we can't always do that alone. Don't have it out with people who are negative and put you down, or put others down. Find the one person you can really talk to, and let off steam. Even though your main problems may not change right away, feeling supported by even one person can give you the strength you need to get through this difficult period.

If you're hanging out with someone who is rebelling, it's likely that you aren't speaking up in your own life. You're letting them act out your feelings for you. You need to take ownership of your feelings and find more positive ways to express them.

Am I self-righteous? Do I feel most powerful after I have been "proven right"? Is it overly important for me to be right all the time? Is it very hard for me to admit any mistakes? Do I criticize other people a lot?

If yes: You need to learn to admit your mistakes. Practice saying, "I'm sorry," and "You're right," to others. Back off a little and learn to relax. Ask yourself why you need to make everyone else wrong to feel good about your own self. Think about what else you have to offer besides criticism.

Do I always think there is something better than what I have? Am I always focused on some golden future? Do I find it hard to appreciate what I have? Am I always envious of what others have? Am I always dissatisfied and letting everyone know it?

If yes: Count your blessings now. Feel proud of your strengths and accomplishments now. Enjoy the moment.

Do I give up when things get tough? If a situation doesn't go the way I want it, do I check out? Do I give up easily? Do I decide everything is wrong with school or my friends the minute things get difficult? Do I find myself often thinking, "Who cares?" and, "It doesn't matter anyway."

If yes: Are you afraid of making a mistake? Do you have really critical parents who never think you've done enough? Or, on the other hand, do you have parents who don't seem to care about your achievements no matter what you do? Giving up on something just because it doesn't come easily right away can mean you are letting *yourself* down. Remember, you are worth it! Don't stay "small" just so you can fit in with your crowd if they are unmotivated types. Setting a goal to achieve something and actually doing it is a big high.

Do any of these feel like YOU?

If yes: Don't think you are a bad person. Don't criticize yourself because you do these behaviors. Now that you recognize them, you can work on making better choices in the future. Write down what you found out on an index card. Keep the card where you can see it to remind you when you are sabotaging yourself.

Don't worry about making mistakes. As Carol says:

Everybody has to learn what works for them and what doesn't. The important thing is to get a sense of who you are, what you stand for, and what you do well. And, this doesn't just happen overnight. Teen years are all about creating an identity. The best identity is someone others feel they can trust, someone who thinks for herself, and someone who makes the world just a little bit better every day.

✤ Be a Hero ✤

"Are you ready? Let's roll."

Those words were spoken by Todd Beamer, one of the people on Flight 93. That's the flight that was hijacked on September 11, 2001, and crashed in a Pennsylvania field. It's believed Todd and other passengers died trying to overpower the hijackers. In doing so, they may have prevented a much greater catastrophe because the terrorists had turned the plane toward Washington, D.C. Since that day, Todd's wife, Lisa Beamer, has given a great deal of thought about what it means to be a hero. Here's what she says:

> Hero. It's a word we hear a lot. You've probably been asked to write an essay about your personal hero. Maybe you wrote about a celebrity or an athlete or someone in history. Maybe you wrote about your mom or dad or a friend. Do you ever wonder if you'll be considered a hero someday?
>
> Most of us don't plan to be a hero. We don't think we'll ever do anything important enough to earn this recognition. My husband, Todd, never thought of himself as a hero. He would be astonished to know that he and his fellow passengers on Flight 93 are regarded today as national heroes because they fought back against the terrorists who hijacked their airplane.
>
> I wonder over and over what enabled these passengers to do what they did on September 11. They were business people, airline professionals, retirees, and college students. There was not a police officer or military person in the bunch. No one had been trained in warfare or weaponry. They didn't

have the skills to take on their hijackers and prevent another mass casualty, but they had the resolve that this was the right thing to do and the courage to follow their instincts.

They had practiced for this moment their whole lives, not by taking classes or entering training, but by making small choices every day where they evaluated the right course of action and then followed through. They were able to become the heroes in the big thing because they were already heroes in the little things

Todd loved country music. One of his favorite songs was by Paul Overstreet called "Heroes." The chorus says, "Heroes come in every shape and size, making special sacrifices for others in their lives. No one gives them medals, the world don't know their names, but in someone's eyes, they are heroes just the same."

Most of us will never be known as a national hero. That's not what we need most anyway. We need lots of us to be heroes in the little things, to make the right choice in each decision we face regardless of cost or consequence. It's a lesson I try to relearn every day.

Do you remember reading the *Peanuts* cartoons when you were little? Charlie Brown would always ask himself if he was going to be the "hero or the goat" of the baseball game. It's a good question to ask as you go through the day, "Am I going to be the hero or the goat?

Be the hero!

⚉ Be Charitable ⚉

Some of the money I make from the sales of this book will go to several charities. Not that I don't like money, myself. But so many people contributed their time and effort to this book—for free. I want to do something to give back, too. I want to be charitable.

Leesa Bellesi is the co-author of *The Kingdom Assignment*. She and a group of high school students—Katie, Terry, Brittany, Sarah, Shannon, Kristy, and Molly—will tell you about adding charity to your life:

Charity: *Generous giving to the poor or to organizations that look after the sick, the poor, and the helpless.*

This is how the dictionary describes something that is an important part of a healthy teenage girl's life. While it's not always fashionable to be a participant in helping others in need, it's an important part of being a well-rounded person.

I have witnessed firsthand how acts of charity by a single ordinary person, or by a small group of people working together, can change lives. It happened in a whole new way at the church where my husband, Denny, is the senior pastor. One day, our dream of creatively teaching a grand lesson to our congregation became a reality. Denny shocked and surprised the people attending our four weekend services by handing out crisp $100 bills. He handed out twenty-five at each service, for a total of 100 people in all. I watched men, women, and children cry, shake, and smile as they listened to the rules of the assignment Denny had given them. He called it a Kingdom Assignment.

1.   This is not your money; it's God's money. He has entrusted it to you.

2.   You need to invest this money outside the walls of this church.

3.   In ninety days you will need to come back and report what you have done.

Suddenly, there was a buzz around our church. People started thinking differently about their money, about everything. The media picked up on it, and the story went into thousands of papers around the world. NBC's *Dateline* followed the story, as did *People* magazine and *Reader's Digest.* Denny and I wrote a book that tells many of the amazing stories and the extraordinary things that those scared 100 people decided to do with the money that was given to them.

Steve was only 14, but he wasn't too young to make a difference. He found a family that had no table at which to eat their meals, let alone somewhere to do their homework. He bought them a table with his $100.

Michael found a family that had lost two daughters to aplastic anemia just months from each other. His company raised $10,000 to pay funeral costs and help their 16-year-old son who had lost his teeth due to a similar disease.

Kim had a desire to help children. She asked bookstores to match her $100. She now has a warehouse full of children's books to distribute, and she reads to kids in cancer wards to help cheer up their day.

I am happy to say that the original $10,000 has now turned into over $500,000—and we're still counting.

So you can see, charity can have wonderful effects on people's lives. I have the privilege of mentoring a group of seven high school senior girls. I asked them how they have helped others and given of themselves, and what that meant to them.

They all agreed that reaching out to others got them away from their own problems and made their own issues look smaller. It helped them cope with disappointment. The girls give up their spring break to go to Mexico every year to help any way they can—build homes, cut people's hair (really!). When they see the sweet and wonderful looks on the faces of the children that they help with crafts, read a story to, or just sit and hug, they feel an indescribable joy.

They give of themselves, and they give of their money. Some of the money that they take out of their own earnings from allowance or working goes back into helping others in need at Christmas time or anytime they think help is needed. They have come to realize that everything they have belongs to God, and it's important that they can give back in many, many ways. These girls have learned what real happiness is all about.

They made a few suggestions of some good ways to give back without spending money.

- Tutor children at hospitals or foster homes.

- Answer phones at a crisis pregnancy center.

- Simply look in people's eyes and smile.

- Teach dance, art, or something you love to underprivileged children.
- Play music for the elderly at a rest home.
- Babysit for someone who can't afford to hire a sitter.
- As you walk out of a store, be on the lookout for someone who needs help with groceries, like a mom with young children.
- Wash a neighbor's car for free.
- Grocery-shop for a house-bound friend or neighbor.
- Pray for people, and let them know you prayed for them.
- Drop a quick note of encouragement to someone who would never expect it.
- Organize a pick-up-trash competition with friends. The one with the most trash gets taken out for ice cream by the other friends.
- Have pizza delivered to someone who is injured or can't afford it.
- Read books to children in the hospital.

The week after Denny handed out the money, some people came up to him and said, "If I'd only gotten $100, I would have really done something great." He pointed out that maybe they had missed the point. We are all given money and talents that we can use each and every day to help others. That is what we are put on this earth to do: to give to others in proportion to what has been given to us.

What would you do with *your* $100?

◎ Be a Role Model ◎

Cathy Ribb's job is to throw parties—for studios opening new movies and as part of the Young Hollywood Awards, which is sponsored by the magazine she works for, *Movieline*. It's the only awards show to honor younger talent such as James King, Hayden Christensen, Carson Daly, and LeeLee Sobieski. Cathy says:

> I'm surrounded by celebrities. I see how they really are in person, and I see how they treat other people. A lot of girls admire celebrities from afar. But some of your favorite stars, I hate to tell you this, are nasty people and are not what they appear. They've got public relations people who work hard to make you think their clients are likable, when they're really totally different in real life. You just see the public image. And not all stars are good role models.
>
> But don't get discouraged. Many other stars really DO have wonderful qualities. So we're not saying you shouldn't admire celebrities. But it's easy to get into celebrity worship, like you wish you could be just like her. So let's get smarter about the reasons we admire celebrities. Because you know what? There are ways you can be just like some of your favorite celebrities.

Cathy's got her own opinions about which celebrities she admires. Here's Cathy's list of what stars do that you should admire—and that you can emulate yourself:

Be honest. Honesty is crucial. If you aren't honest, you'll get a reputation that you can't be believed. Honesty isn't always easy to find in Hollywood. Lots of people are phony and just tell you what they think you want to hear. One celebrity who's known for being honest is Gwen Stefani. She tells it like it is. If she says something, people trust her.

Treat others well. If you don't care about other people, other people won't care about you. Nobody likes a prima donna. Some stars who act like divas don't understand that people only cater to them because they need their money or their help. People kiss their butts, but it's because they are either scared of these divas or they want to get paid. And who needs that? When these stars aren't at the top of the pack later, nobody is going to be there for them. It's better to earn respect and be known for treating others well. Rachel Leigh Cook comes to mind as a star whom I don't hear saying a bad thing about anyone. Learn from her.

Work hard. We admire stars for their talent. But not all stars are naturally talented. And even talented stars have worked long and hard to get where they are. Getting to the top isn't easy. They sometimes spend outrageously long hours rehearsing, memorizing lines, and working. One star who is known for her work ethic is Sarah Michelle Gellar.

Help others. Help other people—just because. Julia Stiles is very charity-driven. She does many charitable things that she doesn't try to get publicity for, that people don't even know about.

Be resilient. Stars who succeed have learned to be resilient. You always hear stars who were told, "You'll never make it in this business; you have no talent." Even the biggest stars are rejected for parts and they lose the awards. At some point, you'll be rejected; you'll lose, too.

People will try to knock you down. Misery loves company, so if others see you succeeding, they might want to make sure you don't get too far ahead. Lose the people who put down your dreams. If you have a dream, you need to put blinders on and not let anyone talk you out of it.

Stay true to your values. People, especially girls, need to be careful in show business. People try to take advantage of them and make them compromise their values. "If you do such and such, I'll make you a star," they are told. Some girls will give in, hoping they will become famous and rich. It's scary what some girls go through in this business while trying to succeed. But each time you give in and go against your values, you feel more and more worthless. And if you do it once, people expect it from you again and again.

The same applies to your life now. It's important never to let anyone talk you into doing something you're not comfortable with or that goes against your values. If you do, you'll always regret it. Don't ever let anyone treat you with less than you deserve to be treated—which is with respect.

Be confident. You don't have to be born with confidence. You can create it (see page 15). Many stars learn to develop confidence and be comfortable with themselves in any situation. Mandy Moore is a good example. She's a young girl with an amazing amount of confidence in herself, and it comes from being secure in who she is.

Stand up for yourself. Stars need to stand up for themselves, and so do you. When someone gets in your space, stand up for yourself. If you don't, they will smell weakness and be on you like a pack of wolves. If you're getting picked on, it's important to get up your courage and stand up for yourself. Otherwise, they will never stop. Don't take any "yuk" from anyone. If you don't like what someone is saying or doing to you, stand up for yourself until it stops. Don't hesitate to ask for help on this one.

Be a good conversationalist. Some stars look blankly at you when you talk about anything besides them. But if you can talk about a variety of topics, you will be more interesting to others. Julia Stiles is very articulate. She can carry on a conversation on topics such as world events. People like to talk to her because she always has something to offer to the discussion.

Have a sense of humor. It's so important to help you get through life to keep a sense of humor. And people will want to be around you if you're funny. Everyone likes someone with a good sense of humor, who can laugh things off. Sandra Bullock is someone who has a great sense of humor and can laugh at the mistakes she makes.

Enjoy yourself. Stars aren't always having fun and games. Have you noticed how many celebrities have made trips to drug rehab? They're under so much pressure to maintain their good looks and career success. They're under constant pressure to perform. In high school, the popular people aren't always having the most fun either. They face that pressure, too. But it's important to relax and enjoy life. (See page 196 for ways to have more joy.)

Be unique. Don't feel you have to conform. Dance to your own drummer. Have your own personal style. Look at Gwen Stefani; she's her own person. She dresses and acts the way she wants to be. She is an authentic person who doesn't let anyone else try to tell her who to be.

Be more than pretty. In Hollywood, pretty girls are a dime a dozen. It's hard to make it on looks alone. It might get you to a certain point, but looks don't get you to the top. To be pretty and hollow is no accomplishment. You want to be appreciated for who you are and what you have to offer. I mean, what do you want to be known for—your talent or your butt? Admire stars like Natalie Portman, who is a talented actress and is also a student at an Ivy League college. Plus, looks don't always last forever. Once your looks go, you need something to fall back on.

Be humble. Don't make the mistake of thinking you're better than everyone else. When success comes fast when you're young, it's easy for stars to start to believe they're better than everyone else. When the whole world seems to love you, you can get a huge ego. You treat other people like they are inferior. You probably see this in your own school hallways: so-called popular people thinking they're superior and being mean to people who aren't in their cliques.

What happens in high school and in the entertainment industry is the same. Many stars crash as fast as they rise. They're stars when they're teens, but then their career ends, and they end up as nobodies and has-beens. And they've stepped on so many people on the way up that nobody is there for them on the way down. It's the same as in high school.

Some people who are popular—but not well-liked—treat people badly in school. Then they graduate from school and get out in the real world, where their clique doesn't make an ounce of difference. Besides, the people they mistreated often become more successful and have more real friends than they do.

Know what's real. The entertainment industry is a tough business to survive in. It's easy to get out of touch with reality. The stars who do stay grounded have their priorities straight. You can take a lesson from them. These priorities include:

- **Family.** Your family will never let your ego get too big. That's why many stars cite their families as playing such as huge role in their lives. They are people with whom the stars can be themselves.

- **Friends.** True friends are often those who knew them before they were stars. Never drop your true friends for people who might be more popular. Your true friends will love you for who you are, not for your status.

- **Faith.** Your faith will remind you that there are things that are bigger than yourself. And it will remind you of what's truly important.

So next time you are admiring and imitating your favorite celebrities, stop for a minute. Are they really, truly good role models?

Think about what's real and true. What you really should be admiring about them. And imitate that! And then you, too, can be a role model for somebody else.

So now you know!
Are you feeling

- confident?
- cool and comfortable?
- capable?
- in control?
- creative?
- caring?
- more conscious?

Are you feeling GirlWise?
You should be!

Contributor Bios

- Carol Adrienne is the bestselling author of *The Purpose of Your Life*, which Oprah Winfrey called a "must-read." Carol is an internationally known lecturer and workshop facilitator. She has also authored and co-authored several other books. Her books have been translated into more than fifteen languages.

- Brooke Allison is a 15-year-old singer who has one album out and another on the way. She's been called "an extraordinary talent who has been touched by God" by Michael Jackson. Mya said she "has a big powerful voice, incredible range, with soulful delivery." She's also the vocal artist on the Disney video, *Cinderella II*.

- Katie Arons is a Ford plus-size model, and has learned all about beauty, fashion, and self-esteem from the experts. She shares this information in her book, *Sexy at Any Size: A Real Woman's Guide to Dating and Romance* and in her online zine for the *real scene—www.ExtraHiP.com*. Katie is a leader in motivating today's curvy society to looking, living, and feeling better . . . NOW!

- Maria T. Bailey is CEO and founder of www.bluesuitmom.com, which has been featured in *USA Today, The Wall Street Journal,* and other major newspapers. She's the author of *The Woman's Home-Based Business Book of Answers*.

- Jill Bauer is a host on QVC. A California native, Jill has a journalism degree and worked in radio and television before landing her dream job at QVC. It took a year and a half of demo tapes, auditions, résumés, and trips before she got the job, but she says, "QVC makes you be your best."

- Lisa Beamer's husband Todd was on the hijacked Flight 93 September 11, 2001. She is the mother of three children, two boys and one girl. Lisa and her family have founded the Todd M. Beamer Foundation, a charitable foundation that will focus on providing long-term assistance to families, especially with children, which were directly impacted by the terrorist attacks of September 11. Its mission includes Todd's vision for training youth for a better tomorrow. The foundation's Web site is www.beamerfoundation.org.

- Leesa Bellesi is co-author of *The Kingdom Assignment*, and is a successful choreographer and dance instructor. She has consulted on the career development of several Christian music artists and professional dancers. Leesa is also a seasoned speaker.

- Susan K. Bishop specializes in the entertainment, media, and communications search business, recruiting hundreds of senior-level executives for key positions with top companies in the fields of cable, broadcasting, publishing, and new media, including CEOs, COOs, and CFOs.

- Dianna Booher is the author of forty books, including *E-Writing, Communicate with Confidence, The Worth of a Woman's Words,* and *Well Connected.* She's also CEO of Booher Consultants, a communication training firm in the Dallas-Fort Worth metroplex, offering workshops and speeches on writing, oral presentations, interpersonal skills, gender communication, and personal productivity. Her Web site is www.booher.com

- Helynna Brooke has raised four children. She's the executive director of the San Francisco Mental Health Board. She is a member of the Women's Leadership Alliance and is very active with women's and girl's issues and in local politics. Helynna is also the co-creator of the *First Moon: Passage to Womanhood,* a ceremonial kit for celebrating a young woman's first menses.

- Kathy Buckley is known as "America's First Hearing Impaired Comedienne." She is also a four-time (1995-98) American Comedy Award Nominee as Best Stand-up Female Comedienne. She has been a guest on *The Tonight Show* and *The Howard Stern Show,* and has been featured on *Today, Good Morning America, CBS This Morning, Entertainment Tonight, Extra, Inside Edition, Live! With Regis and Kathie Lee, The Phil Donahue Show, Leeza,* and in *People* magazine. Her Web site is www.kathybuckley.com.

- Meg Cabot is the author of *The Princess Diaries* and its sequels, *The Princess Diaries: Princess in the Spotlight, Princess in Love,* and many more to come. The first was made into a Disney movie, starring Julie Andrews and Anne Hathaway. AND she writes *The Mediator* series under the name of Jenny Carroll. She also is the author of *All-American Girl* as well as books for adults. Her Web site is www.megcabot.com. (Meg also is really nice and funny in real life and cranks out more good books in a short period of time than anyone I have ever seen.)

- Elizabeth Carlassare is a Silicon Valley-based writer and editor. She's the author of *DotCom Divas: E-Business Insights from the Visionary Women Founders of 20 Net Ventures* (McGraw-Hill, 2000) and the creator of www.dotcomdivas.net, an online open forum for women Internet entrepreneurs. She can be reached at elizabeth@dotcom divas.net.

- Hillary Carlip is one of the most respected names in the world of teen girls. As author of the 1995 book, *Girl Power: Young Women Speak Out,* Hillary was a pioneer in bringing the voice of the teenage girl into the mainstream. *Girl Power* was selected by the New York Public Library for its prestigious "Best Books for Teens" list and Oprah did an entire hour on the book featuring Hillary and some of the book's teen contributors as guests. Hillary's second book, *Zine Scene: The Do-It-Yourself Guide to Zines,* which she designed herself and co-authored with the award-winning, girl-revered author Francesca Lia Block, won an American Library Association Award. Hillary was co-president, founder, and executive creative director of VOXXY, the highly acclaimed, interactive network for teen girls featuring Jennifer Aniston. Hillary has produced Web sites for major stars and companies. (And her own Web site is truly cool: www.flyhc.com.)

- Vanessa Carlisle is the co-author of *I Was My Mother's Bridesmaid: Young Adults Talk About Thriving in a Blended Family* (Wildcat Canyon Press, 1999). She began belly dancing after four years of performing as a hula dancer. She graduated Phi Beta Kappa with a B.A. in psychology from Reed College in 2001 and currently resides in Hollywood, California, where she teaches creative writing classes and dances professionally.

- Cheli Cerra has done runway work for Calvin Klein as well as modeling and national commercials for Geoffrey Beene, JC Penney, Miller Beer, David's Bridal, and Sheraton Hotels. Her agencies included L'Agence and Act 1. She is now an award-winning educator with more than two decades of experience in public education.

- Carla Nocera Cherry plays bass guitar in The Lovekill, and is an avid music lover. She lives in Cleveland, Ohio, with her husband

Robert, and is the business manager for his band, Ether Net, as well as the New York-based band, Poem Rocket.

- Tian Dayton, Ph.D., is the author of eleven books including *Journey Through Womanhood, It's My Life! A Workout for Your Mind, Affirmations for Parents,* and *Trauma and Addiction: Ending the Cycle of Pain Through Emotional Literacy.* She's a clinical psychotherapist and director of program development for the Caron Foundation. She's appeared on *Geraldo, The Rikki Lake Show, The Montel Williams Show,* and MSNBC. (Tian also is an exceptionally nice and generous person.)

- Catherine Dee is a California-based author of a series of award-winning and empowering books for girls that include *The Girls' Book of Friendship, The Girls' Book of Wisdom, The Girls' Book of Love,* and *The Girls' Guide to Life.* Her Web site is www.deebest.com. (We just did a book signing together and she's really fun. E-mail her if you want a chance to be a part of one of her future books!)

- Gun Denhart is co-founder and chair of the board of Hanna Andersson, a children's clothing catalog company founded in 1983. Each year, Hanna Andersson donates 5 percent of its profits to charities that benefit women and children. For five years, Hanna Andersson has been recognized by *Working Woman* magazine in its annual "100 Best Companies for Working Mothers" because of company policies like a 40 percent child care reimbursement.

- Nicole DeVault is a child, teen, and adult etiquette consultant at the Plaza Hotel in New York City. Her classes include dining, social, and business etiquette. She also does extensive etiquette instruction for children and young adults with special needs. You may contact her at her e-mail address: ndevault1@msn.com.

- Kathy Fagan is the author of the National Poetry Series selection, *The Raft* (Dutton, 1985); the Vassar Miller Prize winner, *MOVING & ST RAGE* (University of North Texas, 1999); and the forthcoming collection, *The Charm* (Zoo Press, 2002). She is currently professor of English at The Ohio State University, where she also co-edits *The Journal.*

- Leah Feldon has been helping people dress well for more than twenty years with her books *Dress Like a Million, Dressing Rich,*

WomanStyle, and *Traveling Light,* and through television shows and magazine articles. A former *Today* show contributor and *PM Magazine* host, she most recently created and hosted her own series for The Learning Channel. Her books have been featured on *Oprah* and the *Today* show. She is currently working as a media spokesperson and personal consultant. Her Web site is www.LeahFeldon.com. Her e-mail is Leah@LeahFeldon.com.

- Fawn Germer is the author of the bestseller *Hard Won Wisdom* and a Pulitzer-nominated investigative reporter who has worked as a Florida correspondent for both *The Washington Post* and *U.S. News & World Report.* She has written for many magazines and newspapers and was an adjunct college professor of journalism. Her Web site is www.hardwonwisdom.com.

- Alyssa Gellatly, age 12, has been on the Girl's Editorial Board of *New Moon: The Magazine for Girls and Their Dreams* for two years. Learn more about *New Moon* and the Turn Beauty Inside Out campaign at www.newmoon.org.

- Timi Gleason is the mom of "KC" (Kristin Cathleen) who is learning to do her own laundry at age 14. Timi is an executive and career coach for business people who want to excel in their lives. To find out more about what Timi does, visit her two Web sites at www.hrce.com and www.executivegoals.com. You can write to Timi Gleason at: tgleason@san.rr.com.

- Isabel González has been the "Trendspotting" editor at *Teen People* for two years. She moved from Atlanta, Georgia, to take the job and loves living in New York, where she thinks almost everybody is a trendsetter. Travel is a big part of her job and she finds nothing more exciting than meeting new people who are creative, innovative, and willing to push the envelope of conventional fashion. *Teen People,* a National Magazine Award–winner for General Excellence, is the first pop culture magazine for guys and girls that focuses on stars, style, and substance. With an editorial mix covering celebrities and entertainment, fashion and beauty, and real teens and their accomplishments, *Teen People* has become one of the fastest-growing launches in publishing history. (Isabel is sooo cool, and a total go-getter girl.)

- Renee Grant-Williams is a well-known voice coach whose clients range from U.S. senators to Faith Hill, Martina McBride, and the Dixie Chicks. She has been the subject of a CBS profile, and has appeared on network, syndicated, and cable television programs, as well as hundreds of radio stations. Renee lives in Nashville and is the proud mother of two teenage cats. For information about her book, *Voice Power*, her Master Class Video Series, or to learn more about the master class programs she presents, go to www.MyVoice Coach.com. (Renee also has the *best* phone voice.)

- Harriet Greenspan has been a casting director for more than twenty years. She has cast for ABC, including many soap operas and movies of the week. She is currently casting pilots for Nickelodeon. She lives in L.A. with her teenage daughter, Nicole. (Nicole's advice is in here, too!)

- Nancy Gruver is the publisher of New Moon Publishing, which includes the popular bimonthly magazine, *New Moon*, and the newsletter, *Daughters*, and the Turn Beauty Inside Out (TBIO) campaign, a celebration of media images that promote healthy behavior for girls and boys and Inner Beauty—the beauty of conviction, caring, and action. TBIO is a counter-balance to the damaging and unhealthy messages about beauty that bombard us all through media, film, and advertising every day. Find out more at is www .newmoon.org. (I've learned from talking to other authors that Nancy has a reputation of being really helpful to everyone whose mission is to help girls! Thanks, Nancy!)

- Marilyn Hall is a professional coach who works with individuals and organizations to create strategies for outstanding performance and greater life satisfaction. She is affiliated with the International Coach Federation, Toastmasters International, Coach University, and Corporate Coach University, and is a volunteer for Teen-Coach.com. Additional information about Marilyn and her coaching practice can be viewed at her Web site, www.MarilynHall.com.

- Candace Hammond is a personal coach, trained at Coach University, and a member of the International Coaching Federation. She specializes in life purpose, life quality, working mothers, fitness, teens, and anxiety and panic. She finds nothing more exciting and satisfying than helping others to find their passion, sense of self, and their life purpose. Her Web site is www.personalpowercoach.com.

- Sherry Handel is a trailblazing publishing entrepreneur who is committed to publishing the voices of young women around the world. She is the CEO and president of Blue Jean Media, Inc., which she founded in April of 2000 "to empower girls and young women to create their own media." Sherry is the author of the new, highly acclaimed book *Blue Jean: What Young Women are Thinking, Saying and Doing*. She is publisher and editor-in-chief of Blue Jean Online, a Web site where young women unite to change the world; and publisher of Blue Jean Press, a book publishing imprint. *USA Today* named Blue Jean "The Thinking Girl's Magazine." Her Web site is www.bluejeanonline.com.

- Katharine Hansen, principal résumé and cover-letter writer for Quintessential Résumés and Cover Letters and content provider for Quintessential Careers, is an author and instructor. Her books include *Dynamic Cover Letters* and *Write Your Way to a Higher GPA*, written with Dr. Randall S. Hansen, as well as *Dynamic Cover Letters for New Graduates*, and *A Foot in the Door: Networking Your Way into the Hidden Job Market*. She also is editor of QuintZine, a free career and job-hunting newsletter.

- Clea Hantman and Keva Marie are the authors of the awesomely fun book *Hey Day! Super Amazing, Funk-da-Crazing, Ultra-Glazing Things to Do, Make and Ponder Every Day* (HarperCollins, 2001). Their next book, *Holidazed*, will be published in 2003. Clea also writes a book series called *Goddesses*. Together, they did a zine called Foxy. Their Web site is www.heydaygirls.com.

- Susan Haworth has over two decades of experience developing, designing, and delivering technical, human relations skills, and new employee training programs for telecommunications, technology, banking and finance, manufacturing and mass communications industries. Susan holds a B.A. in Psychology, an M.Ed. in Counseling, and an M.S. in Management.

- Kathy Henderson is the author of *The Young Writer's Guide to Getting Published* (Writer's Digest, 2001, 6th ed.). The book includes listings for 100-plus markets and contests that accept submissions from kids and teens.

- Brandon Holley is the ultra-cool editor-in-chief of *ELLEgirl* magazine, a teen fashion and beauty magazine that "celebrates an independent attitude with an international flair." The magazine's Web site is ellegirl.com.

- Barkley Hope is a Los Angeles fashion designer and owner of the Melrose Avenue boutique Barkley Hope: Items for a Princess. Her store carries an eclectic collection of global and local fashions. Her Web site is www.barkleyhope.com.

- Erin Jacobson has been in the skin care business for five years. She is currently an esthetician at Ole Henriksen Face/Body Spa: www .olehenriksen.com.

- Ellen A. Kaye is a coach and consultant on effective presentation skills, leadership image development, communication and media skills, and etiquette and manners.

- Kay Keating teaches plumbing clinics and online classes in fixing common toilet problems. She's written for a syndicated show and many magazines. Her Web site is www.toiletology.com.

- Brenda Kinsel is a fashion and image consultant based in Marin County, California. Her books, *In the Dressing Room with Brenda, 40 Over 40,* and her upcoming *Wardrobe Companion* instruct women how to wear what they love and love what they wear. Her Web site is brendakinsel.com.

- Sherrie Krantz is the real live person behind the character Vivian on vivianlives.com. She is the president of Forever (After) Inc., a multimedia consulting company.

- Andrea S. Laplante is the affiliate manager for Fox Sports Net New England. She volunteers for the New England Chapter of Women in Cable and Telecommunications (NEWICT) and worked as the chapter president in 2000. She lives in Plainville, Massachusetts, with her husband and daughter, Ava.

- Elizabeth (Liz) K. Lawner, the co-author of *Getting to Know the Real You,* is 14 years old. She has been offering advice to girls in the *Just 4 Girls* section of the national Girl Scout Web site since 1997.

- Mary Lisanti is the CIO of domestic equities at ING/Pilgrim. Mary has responsibility for overseeing Pilgrim's family of domestic equity mutual funds as well as serving as lead portfolio manager for the Pilgrim Growth Products.

- Donna Lopiano is the executive director of Women's Sports Foundation, a national, nonprofit organization dedicated to promoting and enhancing the sports and fitness experience for all girls and women through educational services, advocacy, and recognition programs. She is a life-long advocate of the benefits of sports participation by girls and women. Her Web site is www.womenssports foundation.org.

- Carolyn Mackler is the author of *Love and Other Four-Letter Words*. Her articles have been published in magazines including *Girl's Life* and *Teen People*. Her second teen novel, *The Earth, My Butt, and Other Big, Round Things* will be published in 2003. (Carolyn is totally fun and from the looks of the title, her new book will be, too!)

- Sherry Maysonave is a widely acknowledged expert in communication, image, and personal empowerment. She is the author of *Casual Power* and the president of Empowerment Enterprises, one of America's leading communication-image firms. Sherry has been interviewed by over 200 TV, radio, and print publications and has assisted tens of thousands of people to reach greater levels of success. Additional information about Sherry and her company's services is available at www.casualpower.com.

- Bunny McCune is a psychotherapist in private practice in Ithaca, New York, and co-author of the book *Girls to Women, Women to Girls*. As a singer-songwriter and creative soul, Bunny leads experiential workshops for women and girls across the country. She is currently writing a new book on "The Intuitive Journey," a model which invites individuals of all ages to take a solo trek into the landscape of their own lives with their soulful intuition as their only guide.

- Laura McEwen is the publisher of *YM* magazine. She is the former publisher of *New Woman* and serves on the board of directors of the Cosmetic Executive Women Foundation and the Fashion Group. *YM* magazine, one of the top-selling publications for teenage girls, is a "diet-free zone," abolishing diet-related material and including more plus-size models. Yea, Laura!

- Lisa Miree is Miss Black USA 2002. She is using her title to promote a particularly challenging platform—abstinence before marriage. A producer for an ABC affiliate station in Cincinnati, Lisa is also a singer, dancer, and creative writer. She has a B.S. in Journalism and an M.A. in International Affairs. The Miss Black USA Web site is www.missblackusa.org.

- Harriet S. Mosatche, Ph.D., is the author of three popular books for preteens and teens. Her latest (co-authored with her daughter Elizabeth K. Lawner) is *Getting to Know the Real You: 50 Fun Quizzes Just for Girls* (Prima, 2002). She has also written *Girls: What's So Bad About Being Good? How to Have Fun, Survive the Preteen Years, and Remain True to Yourself* (Prima, 2001), and *Too Old for This, Too Young for That! Your Survival Guide for the Middle-School Years* co-authored with Karen Unger. In addition, Harriet and her daughter Liz are online advice columnists for Girl Scouts of the USA (www.girlscouts.org). The section, *Ask Dr. M,* receives thousands of letters each year from girls around the world. Harriet is also the director of program development for Girl Scouts of the USA. (Another really nice person, with awesome mother–daughter bonding skills.)

- Rachel Muir was 26 years old when she launched her own business with $500 and a credit card, determined to empower girls in math, science, and technology. Almost five years later, the organization, Girlstart, launched the first and only Girls' Technology Center in Texas, and Rachel has raised close to two million dollars. But most importantly, in the last three years, she has helped make hundreds of young women stronger, smarter, sassier, and more assured of a challenging, rewarding future in math, science, and technology. She is a proud recipient of Oprah's Use Your Life Award and numerous other awards.

- Andrea Mulder-Slater is an artist, art educator, and art history writer who lives with her family in St. Andrews, Nebraska. She has worked as a writer, editor, and educational consultant on various art and art history projects including KinderArt.com and Art History.About.com.

- Mariah Burton Nelson is an author and professional speaker who uses sports stories to show people how to lead and succeed with courage and confidence. She can be reached through her Web site: www.MariahBurtonNelson.com.

• Dawn Nocera is the founder and director of EducatingJane.com and ScienceClubMonthly.com. She lives in Columbus, Ohio, with her husband and daughter Annamarie, and is currently awaiting the arrival of a baby boy.

• Lynda Orban is a senior career advisor with CareerBuilder, Inc. She is responsible for analyzing trends in the workplace and tracking the opinions of U.S. workers. The Web site is www.career builder.com.,

• Melissa Palmer is 23 and grew up in Malibu, California. A beauty product junkie, she works with her mother, Jenefer, at Osea skincare, the natural marine-based skincare company they launched together. For more info about Osea, check out www.oseaskin.com.

• Jayne Pearl is a freelance business writer/editor and speaker, and author of *Kids and Money: Giving Them the Savvy to Succeed Financially*. She is a regular commentator on PRI's Marketplace Radio and a contributor to *Family Business* magazine. Her Web site is www.kidsandmoney.com.

• Cait Pomeroy is the founder and former owner of Book Ends, a rare, used, and out of print bookstore located in Lake Jackson, Texas. She is a cookbook author and has published numerous articles and columns for the *Houston Chronicle*. Her Web site is www.us victorygardens.com.

• Congresswoman Deborah Pryce represents Ohio in the U.S. House of Representatives. She is Republican Conference Vice-Chairman for the 107th Congress, making her the highest-ranking Republican woman in the United States House of Representatives. She is a former judge and prosecutor. She has been instrumental in the Child Abuse Prevention and Enforcement Act and The Afghan Women and Children Relief Act, and is involved in efforts to help children with cancer and ensure physician training at children's hospitals. In 2001, Congresswoman Pryce had the honor of being inducted into the Ohio Women's Hall of Fame for her outstanding achievements in public service. Her Web site is www.house.gov/pryce.

- Catherine Ribb has been in the entertainment business for eighteen years and is currently the advertising manager for *Movieline,* a Los Angeles-based celebrity lifestyle magazine. She also owns her own business, Great New You, located on the Web at www.great newyou.com.

- Kathy Roberts is listed in the American Powerlifting Association's Women's Top 20 for 2000. She has set several world, regional, American, and state records in four different Lifetime Drug Free weight classes. Kathy has been ranked as *Powerlifting USA*'s top 20 female powerlifters for the last eight years. She has been featured in *Sports Illustrated* and as an unsung hero on Fox's "Faces of Courage." Kathy's Web site is www.giftofstrength.com.

- Robin Fisher Roffer is president of Big Fish Marketing, Inc., and the author of *Make A Name For Yourself: 8 Steps Every Woman Needs to Create a Personal Brand Strategy for Success.* (Her book really inspired me, so I hunted her down for this.)

- Geneen Roth is author of several books, including *Feeding the Hungry Heart, When Food Is Love, Breaking Free, Why Weight, When You Eat at the Refrigerator, Pull Up a Chair,* and *Appetites.* She has appeared on many national television and radio shows including *Oprah, The Roseanne Show, Good Morning America, The View, 20/20,* and *The NBC Nightly News.* Her work has been featured in numerous publications including *Family Circle, New Woman, Ms., TIME, Cosmopolitan, The New York Times, The Chicago Tribune,* and *The Philadelphia Inquirer.*

- Jennifer Roy is the author of more than twenty educational books, including *Romantic Breakups* and *Difficult People.* Her latest book is *Saratoga: The Family Place to Be.* A former teacher of gifted and talented programs, she's also my identical twin sister. She's now doing the most important job of her life, being a stay-at-home mom to Adam.

- Atoosa Rubenstein is the editor-in-chief of *CosmoGIRL!* She started as an intern at *Sassy* and moved up to fashion assistant at *Cosmopolitan* where she had to keep the fashion closet neat and tidy. She now thinks of *CosmoGIRL!* as "a club for girls, where you can come and talk about whatever issues are on your mind." (Everyone seems to know her, many people said to me the exact same thing: Did you interview Atoosa? You HAVE to!")

- Padi Selwyn is the co-author of *Living Your Life Out Loud: How to Unlock Your Creativity* and *Unleash Your Joy*. She is a professional speaker, and mother of teenage sons. Her e-mail address is padi speaks@hotmail.com.

- Lisa Serantes is the director of incentives at the Express World Headquarters. She began working for Express during her last year at college, where she studied fashion merchandising. Lisa is responsible for planning all the fabulous events that Express throws, as well as conceptualizing motivational techniques for store associates. She has been married for ten years and has an adorable 3-year-old son.

- Aliza Sherman is the original Cybergrrl and author of several books for women about the Internet. Named by *Newsweek* as one of the "Top 50 People Who Matter Most on the Internet," Aliza is a cyber-celebrity, online marketing expert, published author, and international speaker. She started the first woman-owned, full-service Internet company, Cybergrrl, Inc., and the first global Internet organization for women, Webgrrls International. She writes the monthly women's column for *Entrepreneur* magazine. She recently spent over a year driving solo around the country in an old RV. You can check out the free personal site she made using the directions she gives in *GirlWise* at www.geocities.com/rvgirl2.

- Marci Shimoff is the author of the *New York Times* bestsellers *Chicken Soup for the Women's Soul, Chicken Soup for the Mother's Soul 1 and 2,* and *Chicken Soup for the Single's Soul.* She is the president of the Esteem Group, which specializes in self-esteem and inspirational programs. Over the last sixteen years, she has delivered seminars and keynote addresses on self-esteem, stress management, communication skills, and peak performance. (Incredible wisdom just rolls off the tip of Marci's tongue, seriously.)

- Linda L. Smith, J.D., Ph.D., is a faculty advisor in the Honors Program at the University of Toledo in Toledo, Ohio. She is author of the literary biography *Annie Dillard*. Linda is the co-creator of the Poems for Peace Project, an international project to collect poems about the September 11 terrorist attacks.

- Karin Snelson has been hauling stacks of books since she was three feet tall. She has worked as an editor in a small children's book publishing house in Minneapolis; been a writer and designer for Archie McPhee Toys; and worked as a freelance writer/editor in Seattle. She was the senior editor of the Children's Books and Teens section of Amazon.com for four years.

- Merrie Spaeth's career started as a teen actress, beginning with *The World of Henry Orient*, the 1964 film she co-starred alongside Peter Sellers and Angela Lansbury. She also worked as a journalist, then she switched to government, first as a special assistant to William Webster, then the director of the FBI. In 1984, she became director of media relations at the White House for President Ronald Reagan. Several years later, she founded Spaeth Communications, a Dallas-based firm providing communication training and consulting for major companies. Spaeth is also known for doling out the annual Bimbo Awards, which honor the year's best communications gaffes.

- Elaine St. James has been hailed as the leader of the simplicity movement by *The New York Times* and championed as a role model by Oprah Winfrey. The author of the international bestseller *Simplify Your Life*, which detailed how she scaled back her own life in the early nineties, Elaine has written five other best-selling books on simplifying, including *Inner Simplicity, Simplify Your Christmas, Simplify Your Life with Kids*, and *Simplify Your Work Life*. Elaine has appeared on *Oprah, Good Morning America*, CNN, ABC, and NBC News Specials, and National Public Radio, among numerous other national and international radio and television shows. Her books have sold more than 2.5 million copies and have been translated into twenty-seven languages.

- Bonnie St. John has always thrived in situations where the path ahead is not clearly marked, and the competition is intense. She used imagination and determination to become an Olympic Silver Medalist, a Rhodes Scholar, an award-winning IBM sales rep, a White House official, and founder of her own business. She's the author of *Succeeding Sane* (Simon and Schuster, 1998).

- Barbara Stanny is a journalist and former syndicated columnist and career counselor. She is the coauthor of *Choosing and Managing Fi-*

nancial Professionals: A Guide for Women Investors and *How to Be Happily Employed.* She has discussed women and money on CNBC, MSNBC, ABC, CNBC, CNN, *Good Morning America, Maury, The Roseanne Show,* and *The O'Reilly Report, The View,* PBS, NPR, and hundreds of other radio and TV programs. She has also been quoted in stories in *The New York Times, USA Today,* and *Business-Week.* She lives in Washington. Barbara has just finished another book titled, *Secrets of Six-Figure Women: Surprising Strategies to Up Your Earnings and Change Your Life.* (Barbara has some really, really good advice and is really, really generous with it!)

- Heidi Elisabet Yolen Stemple is co-author of *Dear Mother/Dear Daughter* and *Mirror Mirror: Forty Folktales for Mothers and Daughters to Share.* Her Web site is www.heidistemple.com.

- Shelly Strazis is a freelance photographer whose work has appeared in magazines such as *Teen, Real Simple,* and *Jump.* Her Web site is www.shellystrakis.com.

- Galit Strugano is the founder of GirLActik, a sparkly makeup line. She started the line when she was a 23-year-old makeup artist in L.A. Her makeup is used by stars such as Destiny's Child, Britney Spears, Julia Roberts, Dream, Eden's Crush, and others. It regularly sells out at department stores and L.A. boutiques. Her Web site is www.girlactik.com. (Galit wins the award for referring me to the most interviewees in this book. She is extremely cool and very fun.)

- Kelly Tanabe won enough scholarships to leave Harvard debt-free and her parents guilt-free. She is the award-winning co-author of *Get Free Cash for College, Money-Winning Scholarship Essays and Interviews, Get Into Any College,* and *Accepted! 50 Successful College Admission Essays.* She also tours the country speaking with parents and students about getting into and paying for college. On her Web site, www.supercollege.com, you can search a free scholarship database and apply for the SuperCollege.com Scholarship.

- Sarah Thomas-Fazeli is a writer and mind–body specialist based in Los Angeles. She holds an MFA from the California Institute of the Arts and currently teaches yoga and Pilates in a variety of settings.

- Joan Tinnell loves her job and is thrilled to wake up every day and get started. She recently opened a new spa called Spahhs, in Chicago.

Joan has been in the spa and beauty business for twenty years and owned a spa with 6,000 clients. She puts her heart and soul into pampering people and making them feel good about themselves.

- Melva "Nikki" van Schyndel, naturalist and artist, teaches at the WOLF School of Natural Science in Washington State and British Columbia. She is a lead instructor during WOLF Camps for teens and adults, teaching skills of the naturalist, tracker, herbalist, survivalist, and scout. Her Web site is www.WolfJourney.com.

- Jennifer Walsh is president and editor-in-chief of The Beauty Bar and www.thebeautybar.com. Her experience as an artist spans runway, print, and television. She hosts her own monthly beauty segment on CBS (Florida).

- Stephanie Walter Williams is a documentary film producer and director who specializes in music and human interest stories. She works as both a "gun for hire" and independently. Stephanie and her husband, John, also work with the Prospect Park YMCA in Brooklyn, New York, passing on their documentary story telling secrets to local teens, who are working to create their own docs. Stephanie's passion for film-making comes from her creative parents, Kurt and Maryanne, and she credits her first best girl friend, Kathy Meagher, for giving up the popular girls to help Stephanie put on her backyard theater productions.

- Susie Wang is the heart and soul of Aqua Dessa Spa Therapy. Susie and her boyfriend, Byung Kim, started Aqua Dessa when they were in college. Her products are made with the highest quality, organic pure ingredients and no chemicals. Her Web site is www.aqua dessa.com. (Susie is a *phenomenal* role model. I was so impressed with Susie when I met her that we are now working on a project together—stay tuned!)

- Rachel Weingarten is a New York City–based celebrity makeup artist and the co-founder of PlanetPretty.com, the number one beauty/lifestyle site on the Internet for teens and young women. Rachel is a frequent contributor to many women's magazines and Web sites. Rachel is an expert on teen beauty and trends, and one of the founders of AMPLIFYonline, a marketing and promotions company, specializing in teen- and women-friendly marketing campaigns. Rachel is also the founder and executive director of Good To Know, Inc. (GTK Group) a nonprofit organization that produces free health information and resources for teens including HealthSquad.com, a cool health, fitness, and nutrition Web site for teen girls and young women. (I met Rachel in Brooklyn and she and her sister are both really nice. We had a lot in common, all being daughters of Holocaust survivors.)

- Rebecca "Kiki" Weingarten is the director of the Integrated County Plan for the Department of Youth and Community Development for the City of New York. Rebecca is a trained psychoanalyst who taught in the New York City Public School System and created programs for adolescents including Authorship and Authority, empowering youth through journal writing. She is also a produced playwright whose works have been performed off-Broadway, and an author of children's books, including *I Touched the Moon*. (Kiki is the sister of Rachel!)

- Jane Yolen is an author of children's books, fantasy, and science fiction. She is also a poet, a teacher of writing and literature, and a reviewer of children's literature. She has been called the Hans Christian Andersen of America and the Aesop of the twentieth century. Jane Yolen's books and stories have won the Caldecott Medal, two Nebula Awards, two Christopher Medals, the World Fantasy Award, three Mythopoeic Fantasy Awards, the Golden Kite Award, the Jewish Book Award, and the Association of Jewish Libraries Award. Her Web site is www.janeyolen.com.

Index

1989

About Julia DeVillers

Also the author of: *Teen girlfriends: Celebrating the good times, getting through the hard times.* It's part of the *New York Times* bestselling *girlfriends* series. And co-author of *You Can Make It Big Writing Books: A Top Agent Shows You How to Develop a Million-Dollar Bestseller.*

Job: Freelance writer and mom.

Before that: Editor-in-chief of an educational publishing company.

Lives in: Columbus, Ohio.

Married? Yup, to David. I met him when I was 17. He's a gang prosecutor now.

Kids? Yup, five-year-old daughter, Quinn, and two-year-old son, Jack.

School stuff: M.A. in journalism from The Ohio State University and a B.A. in communications from the State University of New York at Oswego. And a high school diploma from Colonie High School in Albany, New York.

Best known in high school for: Being an identical twin.

Most embarrassing moment: See page 10.

Favorite things about writing *GirlWise*: Meeting so many of the people from all over the country featured in this book. And being genuinely inspired by every single person who's in it!

Website: www.girlwise.com.

Email: Julia@girlwise.com. E-mail me to hear about how to be in my future books!

A Girl's Guide to Growing Up

Being a girl is a lot of fun *most* of the time. But some days are really difficult. Dealing with a body that is changing before everyone's eyes, increasing amounts of schoolwork, boys, other girls, friends, makeup, clothing, parents. Wow! Life as a preteen or early-teen girl can be tough, and that's why every girl has questions about growing up. This book is your guide to surviving those trying times and feeling good about yourself in the end. You'll find some great ways to handle emotional issues and deal with daily crises as you discover how to:

ISBN 0-7615-3289-7 / Paperback
240 pages / U.S. $12.95 / Can. $19.95

- Develop a positive self-image
- Maintain healthy relationships with parents, friends, and boys
- Deal with peer pressure, bullies, brats, and violence
- Dream big and turn those dreams into reality
- And much, much more!

Cool Quizzes and Hot Tips About Growing Up

Find out about your friends and yourself—who you are, what you like or don't like, and how you can become the person you want to be. This book shows you how, with clever quizzes and creative tips about emotions, self-esteem, family and friends, school, boys, and more!

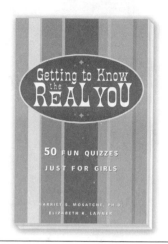

ISBN 0-7615-2954-3 / Paperback
240 pages / U.S. $12.95 / Can. $19.95

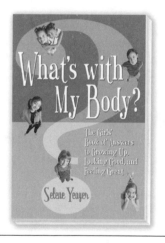

All About Girls, Puberty, and Growing Up

Reassuring and accurate advice for all preteen and young teen girls (and their parents) is presented in a handy question-and-answer format. All the toughest and most important stuff that's on your mind is right here, from body changes, skin and hair care, and menstruation to moods, eating disorders, and sexuality. You'll discover what your body is all about and feel great about it and yourself!

ISBN 0-7615-3723-6 / Paperback
272 pages / U.S. $12.95 / Can. $19.95

Prima's Popular A GIRL'S WORLD Series:
Real-Life Advice for Preteen and Early-Teen Girls

ISBN 0-7615-3295-1

ISBN 0-7615-3292-7

ISBN 0-7615-3294-3

ISBN 0-7615-3290-0

ISBN 0-7615-3291-9

ISBN 0-7615-3293-5

Paperback / U.S. $12.95 / Can. $19.95

Produced in conjunction with the team of volunteer girl editors at A Girl's World Productions, Inc., its Web site, www.agirlsworld.com, and girls all around the world, these indispensable books contain real advice for girls by girls.